This is **your** opportunity to
build something extraordinary.

*The question is, will **you** seize it?*

1

Title: Professional Follow-Ups: Mastering the Art of Staying Connected
Author: Howard Philpott
Publisher: SMARTEFFORTS FZ LLC
ISBN: 979-8-89686-280-2

Disclaimer: This book is intended to provide general information and practical tips on follow-up communication strategies. The author and publisher assume no responsibility for errors or omissions, or for outcomes resulting from the use of the information provided. The advice in this book should not replace professional guidance tailored to individual situations.

Trademarks: All brand names, trademarks, and registered trademarks mentioned in this book are the property of their respective owners and are used for reference purposes only. The inclusion of such trademarks does not imply affiliation with or endorsement by the trademark holders.

Printed in: United Kingdom

First Edition: March 2025

For more information, visit: howardphilpott.com/follow-ups

Dedicated to:

Jane, my soulmate, my everything,
without whom my world would have no light

James and Matthew, our boys who have
grown into wonderful young men

George, whose mischievous and loving spirit;
hugs and guides me daily

and to

All those, whose repeated successes
and failures enabled this book to exist

A special thank you to:
Andy, Rhian, Tony and Nichola whose prompt
proofing made a ridiculously tight deadline possible.

*To mum and dad without your loving guidance
nothing would be possible*

Distilled Wisdom

If this is the only page you read, its wisdom has the power to transform your life — if you choose to adopt it and **act on it**.

"Don't let your learning lead to knowledge; let your learning lead to action." – Jim Rohn

"Formal education will make you a living; self-education will make you a fortune." – Jim Rohn

"Your business grows in direct proportion to your personal growth." – Don Failla

"Prospecting is sorting, not convincing." – Don Failla

"We don't sell; we educate and offer solutions." – Big Al

"If you want to be successful in network marketing, you need to master the art of storytelling." – Eric Worre

"People join people, not businesses." – Big Al

"The fortune is in the follow-up." – Eric Worre

"Success is neither magical nor mysterious. Success is the natural consequence of consistently applying the basic fundamentals." – Jim Rohn

"The speed of the leader determines the speed of the pack." – Eric Worre

"You can't say the wrong thing to the right person, and you can't say the right thing to the wrong person." – Big Al

"Network marketing is not about selling; it's about sharing an opportunity." – Don Failla

Table of Contents

Introduction to "Professional Follow-Ups"

In a world where opportunities are often fleeting, mastering the art of the follow-up can be the difference between stagnation and remarkable success. *Professional Follow-Ups* is your guide to transforming casual interactions into meaningful connections, and one-time customers into lifelong advocates.

Whether you're a seasoned professional or just beginning your journey, this book equips you with actionable strategies, proven techniques, and a mindset shift that will elevate your approach to follow-ups.

Expect to uncover the secrets of effective communication, timing, and personalisation. Discover how to nurture relationships without becoming overbearing, and how to stay top-of-mind without resorting to clichéd tactics.

The benefits?

Increased trust, better conversion rates, and a reputation as someone who genuinely cares — a rare and valuable trait in today's fast-paced world.

This book will empower you to:

- Build authentic connections that last.
- Overcome common fears and hesitations about following up.

- Utilise tools and templates for efficient and impactful communication.
- Develop a system for follow-ups that ensures no opportunity slips through the cracks.

The techniques in *Professional Follow-Ups* aren't just theories — they're field-tested and proven to work. By implementing the strategies within, you'll not only improve your professional relationships but also enjoy the tangible benefits of increased sales, stronger networks, and the satisfaction of knowing you've mastered one of the most crucial skills in any industry.

Five benefits you will gain.

- **Build Confidence in Communication:** Learn practical strategies to overcome fear and hesitation, making follow-ups feel natural and stress-free.

- **Strengthen Relationships:** Discover how consistent and thoughtful follow-ups can help you nurture stronger, more meaningful connections with prospects, clients, and colleagues.

- **Master Time Management:** Develop an organised and efficient follow-up system that saves time while maximising results.

- **Increase Success Rates:** Apply proven techniques to improve your response rates and turn more prospects into loyal customers or partners.

- **Stand Out as a Professional:** Gain insights into creating a positive and lasting impression, positioning yourself as trustworthy and reliable in any business setting.

Above all you will discover that success does not require natural talent when you consistently follow a proven system.

About the Author

Howard Philpott was born in Splott, Cardiff, a suburb built in the late 1800s to provide affordable housing for dock workers and the burgeoning steel and coal industries.

From these humble beginnings, Howard's life took an extraordinary trajectory. In the 1992 General Election, he was the UK's youngest parliamentary candidate for the governing party.

He served as a special advisor and part of a ground-breaking central office by-election campaigning team. His innovative approach brought personalisation to mass campaigning, setting new standards in political strategy.

Howard's ability to influence was evident even as a child. "Come and ask my mum — she'll let me go if you ask," was a refrain that showcased his early knack for persuasion.

This book is a testament to Howard's journey of transformation and growth.

Despite being the only pupil in his school to be thrown out of English Literature at O-Level — a compulsory subject at the time — Howard defied the odds. His teacher famously called him "a bloody waster," yet at 58, he has overcome his lifelong struggle with writing and spelling to author his first book.

Howard once quipped, "If I went to a posh school, I'd be labelled dyslexic, but here it's just that I can't spell."

His journey from reluctant student to published author is a powerful reminder that change, and development are always possible.

Howard's career spans diverse roles in business and management, and he is a part-qualified accountant. However, his true passion lies in helping others realise their potential.

He has spoken at numerous national conferences and select events in dozens of cities across four continents for several global companies, earning the title of "Chief Inspirational Officer" from a Global VP of one multi-billion-dollar corporation.

A number of the people Howard has mentored have gone on to achieve remarkable success, winning global and national company-wide awards, as well as national trade and association honours.

His ability to bring out the best in others has made him a sought-after mentor and speaker.

Howard possesses a rare ability to help others see solutions to their challenges and to paint vividly emotional, inspiring pictures that motivate action.

His personal journey and professional expertise make him uniquely qualified to guide you through the transformative power of professional follow-ups

How to use this book

Use it as a skeleton, a framework for you to flesh out.

"Done always smashes perfect"

Stop waiting for the "right" time or for when you know enough. Just start and improve as you go along.

Don't use a disagreement around a tiny detail as your reason for procrastination – Let me explain with an example, I suggest a call on day 5 but you know day 6 suits you better, don't think "this won't work for me" take ownership and do day 6 – The key here is just do it, the specific detail is not important, it will never be an exact science, it will always be a blend of judgement, experience and art.

You don't need to understand, agree with or most of all, like the way people collectively behave – The guidance and tips in this book provide you with the best chance to stay connected to them long enough to exert a positive influence.

Ask any gambler "the house" always wins in the end because they play the longer-term odds. They never change the plan just because of one single outcome. Follow the system consistently and you will get the results.

Part 1

The Mindset of Follow-Up

Chapter 1: A Non-Negotiable Foundation

"The foundation of successful follow-ups will always be found in following a process, not in natural ability"- **Howard Philpott**

For us in our industry, the "follow-up" is where the rubber meets the road, it is where we succeed or fail. There are no short cuts to this section, there are ways to improve, to become better. There is absolutely no way to avoid this section if you wish to build a great business.

It is worth noting that this is the only part of the recruitment section that can be neither outsourced nor overlooked. You just have to find a way. You must work out, your way to just do it.

Let me be clear, if you do not find a way to professionally follow-up prospects and lead your team to do the same, your business will NEVER, EVER reach its potential and you will constantly be questioning its worth.

No Follow-ups = No Prosperity

Again, for clarity and repetition:
No Follow-ups definitely means there will be No Prosperity

It's worth noting that although many of the skills or traits of professional follow-ups are identical to "sales". There is always one key difference we must bear in mind, that is we are not "selling" the opportunity we are looking to **promote** it, and more specifically as professionals we seek to promote it in a way that personally resonates with each individual prospect.

Our role is to highlight and tailor the opportunity, so our prospect feels it was created just for them.

Did you know luxury brands like BMW, Google, L'Oreal and Apple invest constantly in sales training; they treat it as a science, in fact they spend millions and millions every single day to refine and improve their process.

They are data driven, for example Apple staff in stores do 40 minutes of training per day. Think about that, every shift you'd log on and do 40 minutes of training to improve. You and I both know that Apple are successful at "knowing what people want" – Do you think they would continue to invest at that level if they were not certain it was worth it?

Think about this for a minute, with all these resources Apple feel the business will be more successful if their store staff do 40 minutes of training **each** shift. I am not for one moment seeking to downplay the role but to state an obvious fact, these are retail assistants, working in a shop that has a very limited range of products. Take some time to reflect on your role in contrast. Your role is to promote an opportunity that changes lives, you have an almost infinite range of possibilities.

18

The single question I want you to consider as you reflect is:

How many minutes training and personal development have you personally done in the past 7 days?

Please write your answer in the box below:

☐ Minutes

Notice how small the box is? There is a brilliant story from Jim Rohn, where he talks about someone, he was coaching to become more successful, he had already identified the problem.

A simple lack of calls. He instructed the person he was helping to write the number of calls in a box "You'll see it's a very small box; I did that deliberately, it means you can only fit a number in it, there is no space for all the excuses you might wish to use. The only thing you can fit into the box is the one thing that matters, when it comes to determining the scale of your success. And that is the raw, naked number "

Now you know why the box above is so small.

How many minutes, do you think a professional would have done to hone their skills?

Personally, I spend about 60-80 minutes a day getting better at the basics of our industry.

A great tip, reach out to five people you admire and ask them how much time they invest in themselves. Success leaves clues, so go out and hunt for them and when you find them, make sure you follow them.

It is vitally important that you think of this effort to become better and improve your effectiveness as an investment rather than a chore.

One of the most pleasurable consequences of getting better at what you do, is the fact that you start to accrue wisdom. Once you feel the thrill of being able to help your team by sharing the wisdom you've built up, it becomes addictive.

One of my favourite Jim Rohn quotes *"If You Work Hard on Your Job, You Can Make a Living. If You Work Hard on Yourself, You Can Make a Fortune"*

Returning to the list of amazingly successful companies, let's take a quick look at Google. Who has ever done paid adverts with Google?

Ask yourself this question, is there any company on the planet that has more information on you, your business and your industry than Google? Are Google one of the most cutting-edge technology companies?

My last question on Google, for those who have bought ads from them, did they offer to "help" you get more success from your ads?

Did you have someone reach out to schedule an appointment to "improve" your results? This is a WAKE-UP moment. If Google still feel the professional human follow-up is worthwhile, why are you so attached to your view that it's okay to avoid it?

It's time to be more professional in your follow-up!

Here's the first tip – Professionals do not do "chitty – chats". It may look like a friendly random chitty chat but as professionals they are going through a rehearsed process to get that sale.

Successful professionals understand that if a sale (or in our case a decision to join) is made when a prospect has three things come together.

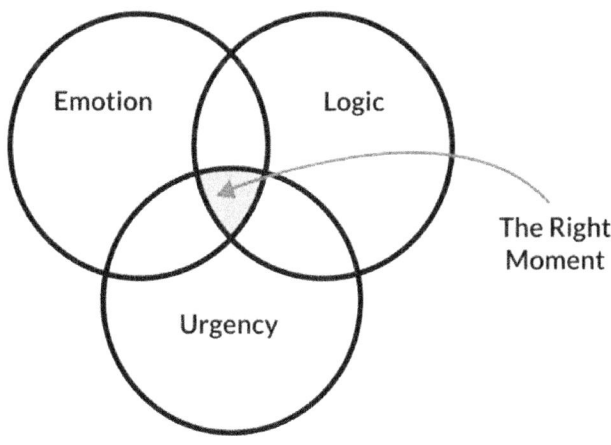

They have an emotional attachment to what they are buying, when they see clear logical proof it will be beneficial, and when they have some sense of urgency concerning what they are about to buy or sign up for.

When you are juggling those three separate spheres of, emotion, logic and urgency in a conversation you need to be consciously focused on each of them at the same time whilst still having the brain capacity to also hold focus on the next words you will say.

Professionals are able to make this look simple. In contrast amateurs struggle to string a coherent sentence together and fail to keep an eye on the three key emotional needs, so they drop one or two and miss out on a great potential recruit.

Now amateurs justify the difference in success with comments like, "it's okay for her, it just comes naturally, or I've never been good at talking to people."

Well, I have to tell you this is a load of crap. There is a difference, and it is a warranted difference in outcomes, and it is due to the amount of effort to get better that these professional people have devoted to this skill during their lifetime.

Right now, you are reading this book with what I can only assume is a burning desire to get better, to improve your income and transform your lifestyle.

So, here is the key tip for you: Invest in rehearsing these conversations, then go and find 100s or better 1,000s of prospects to practice on, then critically review each one to work out how you could have handled it better or said something in a different way.

This is the only way to get better and build a big business. **IMPORTANT NOTE:** When I say professional, I definitely don't mean you should be stiff, formal and pompous. Your personality should shine through, you should always be authentic.

However, during the "sales" process you need to be authentically focused on showcasing your professionalism.

This is only accomplished if you put in the hard yards to become competent in these key areas of following up:

- Develop the correct mindset
- Understand the follow-up process
- Rehearse the phrases and answers
- Create the tools you'll use
- The most critical is creating the "full picture" and showing it to your prospect, in a way that allows them to see a bright future is within their grasp.
- The awareness of how to keep the pot bubbling

We will cover these six points in greater detail in the coming chapters, but first we need a frank discussion about you, more specifically, about how much momentum you have currently.

Chapter 2: Building the Right Mindset

First, I just want to establish we have never met (well maybe I have had the absolute pleasure of saying hello to a few of you) but for the sake of this piece let's agree that we've never met.

Despite that fact, I would be prepared to take an educated punt at how you are feeling as you read this book. I am pretty sure that the following three traits all apply to you right now:

- o **You are not work shy.**
- o **You feel you should have achieved more by now.**
- o **You begin to think real success is not meant for you.**

How close was I?

No, I don't have a crystal ball, but I do have 4 decades of practical experience of working with 1,000s of authentically ambitious people.

Let me now focus on some traits that might well be a symptom of why you are being held back from achieving the true potential your business could have. We need to have a frank and meaningful conversation! Yes, you and me, right now!

When I'm about to have a challenging conversation like we are about to have on the next page, for example when I'm doing 1-2-1 coaching sessions.

Before I go "all gung-ho on them." I give them the "sentence". This is to help position (and soften) what's about to come. It is an attempt to limit the shock that people often experience when hearing true constructive feedback for the first time.

So, to help you (from getting all indignant), please read the following sentence carefully. I do need you to help me out slightly, so please fill in the bold bits in the following paragraph with the appropriate words.

"You know I am fully committed to helping you achieve **(your #1 goal),** and you have seen how much support I have given, such as when I **(insert example of active support)** so you know what I am about to share with you comes from a place of (**support, care or love**). My role is to help you improve the skills you need to succeed not just the ones you enjoy doing. So here is what I would like you to reflect upon."

Then I let them have "both barrels" in a clear and concise way. The problem that is creating the hold-up is always a mix of these two issues:

a) *You are not generating enough new prospects*
b) *You are not even following up the few prospects you have professionally*

Now for the next ten minutes or so, we trudge through all the excuses, feeble justifications, until we get to, and be in no doubt we always get to the "I know" moment.

This is where I celebrate, because at this moment the person I am working with is ready to make a simple, although not easy change, to their business that will transform their future forever.

Here is the great news I give them. You are in exactly the right place at the right time to unlock the success you aspire to, the detailed path to achieve that success will be provided shortly. However, there are a few areas where you will need to "get your shit together, right now."

These are non-negotiable, there are no shortcuts, there is no VIP access to skip the line. Without an unshakeable commitment to improving in these areas, you will continue to have the unsatisfying level of success you have experienced in your life up to this point.

Again, we are not looking for immediate perfection, you will not wake up tomorrow and be a changed person, this is a process. It is a long and challenging process where you will have periods where you take 2 steps forward and 6 steps backwards. So, the commitment you must make is this:

"I promise myself and my family that every day I will do my very best to improve my chances of success – If in my assessment I fall short today, I will reset and renew my commitment tomorrow because mine and my families' true freedom is worth the effort."

Chapter 3: Breaking Through Stuckness

Here's the real surprise, and it's a revelation that took me decades to discover.

The lack of prospecting. The woeful attempts at professional follow-ups are not the fundamental issue here, they are a symptom of the fundamental issue.

When we try to discover the real reason that causes failure amongst people who have everything they need to succeed. We must look deeper. They have the knowledge. They know exactly what they should be doing to follow-up. They have all the skills. They could without doubt pick up the phone and dial the prospect.

They also possess that important, yet sometimes missing ingredient. Not only do they have a desire to succeed, they have a genuine passion to help other people succeed in life.

So, why do they struggle to make it happen?

The real reason is a lack of **FAITH**; they don't fully believe.

They lack faith in almost all these areas:

- Faith in themselves.
- Faith in their opportunity.
- Faith in their company.
- Faith in their prospects.

If you do not see a bright future for yourself in your opportunity, you cannot in all good conscience seek to introduce people to your opportunity, unless of course you are some kind of con artist.

So, you are now mentally conflicted. You want to build a great business, you desperately need to build a great income, but you feel it's not going to be possible. In your mind you know that no one will be prepared to put up with the struggle that's needed.

This puts our brains in a real pickle, a passionate desire coupled with a complete lack of faith pulling in opposite directions.

This is the real reason people struggle with follow-ups, our primitive brain desperately wants to avoid this mental struggle because it uses so much energy, it cannot directly stop the desire, but it can and indeed does create so many reasons why it won't work (the brain loves a negative more than anything else). This is why you have so many negative thoughts running through your head.

If this chimes with you, then right now you need to find a way to rekindle that almost childlike excitement about your future possibilities. As an experienced coach and mentor, I can tell you that this is the most critical part of my role.

This lack of faith in the future is the most debilitating frame of mind for anyone in Network Marketing, it is like a cancer that grows and I'm sad to say if it's allowed to grow unchecked then in most cases it becomes terminal.

If that's the diagnosis, what is the cure?

So, let me be blunt, there is no simple fix. There is no magic bullet, but I have seen time and time again there is a practical and achievable solution.

This solution will require approximately 90 days of the most committed effort you have ever put into your business.

It has just three clear steps.

1. Choose a single, measurable recruitment goal – This goal must be in line with what a new starter might have, each company, each plan, will be different. You will have a guide for new team members to aim for. I would use something along the lines of - Recruit # people within the next 3 months?

2. Use all of the prospecting methods that your successful upline team advocate – Stop with the "I don't like…." This step clearly says USE ALL – It does not mention use all equally. Treat it like a buffet, a buffet where you MUST try everything! So you are able to talk about each item with authenticity and confidence.

3. Speak about your opportunity / your upline / your company ONLY in positive ways. This is not

censorship; it's just choosing what to focus on. This third-party edification is a fundamental keystone to the MLM industry. If you refer to your company as "shit" or you describe your upline as a "bitch" – Great people will not join you, they will not want that drama in their lives.

4. This is not really 4, it's an extension of 3. Let's call it 3a – speak publicly about your opportunity, as you never have before; hold webinars, Facebook lives, real world events. Offer to be a speaker at other group events such as business networking events, breakfast clubs or other organisations such as Rotary or the Women's Institute.

These are guaranteed to push you out of your current feeling of being trapped and not progressing.

In fact, this is such a common feeling, that I have a nick name for the mental feeling it creates. I call it "stuckness". There is ONLY one treatment to clear this condition.

However, this cure does not work if you go at these three-steps half-heartedly. It can only be a successful treatment if you fully embrace all the steps for at least 90 days, as this is the realistic time frame for creating a new permanent outlook on your business.

Here's my promise to you – if you really commit to making this happen but genuinely lack someone in your life that can give you the emotional support in the form of a much needed "kick up the arse" or the "let me put my arms around you" that you feel you need, then I have a few spaces where I can be that person for you. If, after trying, you absolutely cannot find someone, use this link to join my mentoring program: howardphilpott.com/bookmentoring

Chapter 4: Honest Self-Awareness

No matter what the current situation you find yourself in, you are in a great position to bring about a huge transformation. Improvement is literally around the corner, if you choose to go and find it.

Now, whilst everyone's current situation is unique to them, there are some universal common areas that will help everyone, as they are fundamental to raising belief and faith by increasing effort while simultaneously improving skills.

Here are the three fundamentals to ensure your best future success:

- Honest self-awareness
- Critical reflection
- Willingness to adapt

Your challenge that must be overcome is not in what you can do today, or tomorrow. It's rooted in the fact that you don't see yourself as being worthy of success in the future. It is this unfounded bleak vision, that exists only inside your own head that constantly undermines you.

Do you hear yourself say things like:

"Oh, it's pointless calling them, they won't join, and I won't succeed."

"What's the point of practising those phrases, you can't get people to talk to you anyway."

It is so sad I see many, many truly capable people drive themselves to quit an otherwise great business purely because they lacked faith, the faith that they would need to fall back on when it gets tough and trust me it always gets tough.

There is no real scientific way to help with this because it's faith not proof, all you can do is use the evidence that is all around you to build a positive vision of a possible future.

If others can succeed, then there is no reason that you can't succeed as well, providing you put in the required effort.

Now is the time to have blind faith that it will work, and trust it will be worth the effort. An absence of this blind faith is the root cause of failure to professionally Follow-Up.

So how do you overcome that? It is as simple to explain as it is difficult to action.

Let me cover these 3 areas briefly. In reality I could write a book just about these, they are that important.

Honest Self-Awareness
Why: You can't grow if you don't first understand where you truly stand. Recognising your strengths, weaknesses and blind spots is the foundation for meaningful progress.
How: Be honest with yourself about where you're falling short in

your follow-ups—are you consistent? Do you approach these with confidence or hesitation?

Practical Example: If you realise you procrastinate because you fear rejection, acknowledge it. This awareness lets you shift your mindset and approach each follow-up with purpose.

Critical Reflection

Why: Simply being aware isn't enough; you need to analyse what's working and what isn't. Reflection helps you identify patterns and refine your approach.

How: After each interaction, take a moment to assess; What went well? What could have been better?

Practical Example: If a prospect didn't respond, ask yourself why. Did you follow up too late, or were you hiding behind a text? Or was it simply not the right time for them?

Willingness to Adapt

Why: Growth requires change. Sticking to the same methods when they're not yielding results will only hold you back.

How: Be open to trying new strategies, even if they feel uncomfortable at first.

Practical Example: If your usual texts aren't sparking interest, try a voice note or a quick video message instead. Adapt your approach to what resonates with each prospect

These three work perfectly when done together. Without self-awareness, reflection is shallow and lacks firm foundations. Without reflection, adaptation is aimless. Changes will be down to random luck, if you fail to accurately and objectively reflect the truth. Together, they create a powerful cycle of growth and improvement.

One thing that can massively improve the speed of mastering the skill of professional follow-ups, is to use Directed Practice. By adding directed practice you can quickly jump to the next level.

Directed practice is where you have someone you trust, who also has the right level of experience to provide constructive feedback.

One of the many benefits of this method is the fact that it takes your personal biases out of the situation. It is the only effective way you can identify blind spots you might miss and suggest specific adjustments.

This external perspective accelerates growth by offering insights you can't gain on your own. This illustration provides a great visualisation. It clearly shows how we see things very differently when we are at the centre of things, whilst independent, remote observers get to see the full picture.

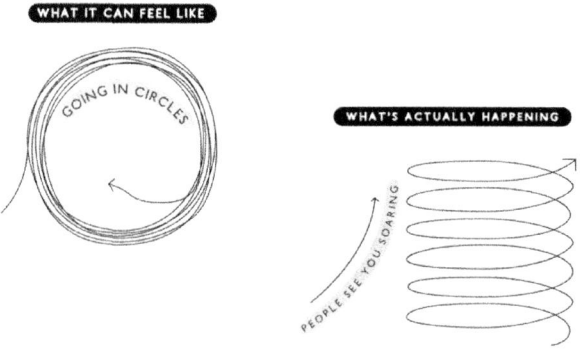

Often people can't handle this process. They don't like to be told where they can improve, they think that any change is pointless as they have always done it this way.

Imagine you're consistently following up with prospects using the same script, but you're not getting responses. Without reflection, you'll continue repeating the same mistake, hoping persistence alone will work.

Now, add directed practice; where a mentor reviews your script, points out that it's too formal and suggests a friendlier, more conversational tone. By making that change, you're far more likely to connect with prospects and see results.

This process is necessary if you wish to become a professional at Follow-Ups.

It is the most efficient and effective way to get better quickly. You owe it to your recruits to be the best you can so you can be the best at helping them. Oh and by the way, a by-product of that improvement will be a huge growth in your business and income.

Part 2

The System and Process of Follow-Ups

Chapter 5: Amateurs and Professionals - The Difference

Let's kick off with some formal definitions:

An **amateur** is someone who engages in an activity, sport, or field of work primarily for pleasure, interest, or personal satisfaction rather than for financial gain or professional commitment.

Amateurs may lack formal training or expertise and often pursue their activity as a hobby rather than as a primary occupation.

Key characteristics of an amateur:

- Works for enjoyment, not financial gain.
- May have limited formal training or experience.
- Pursues the activity on a part-time or casual basis.

A **professional** is someone who engages in a specific activity, occupation, or field of work as their primary source of income and typically possesses advanced skills, training, or qualifications in that area.

Professionals adhere to established standards of practice and often operate within a recognised framework of ethics or regulations.

Key characteristics of a professional:

- Earns income from their work.
- Has formal training, expertise, or certification.
- Maintains a high level of skill and competence.
- Often held to a code of ethics or professional standards.

Now everyone has the ability to choose whether they conduct their business like an amateur or a professional. Indeed, I would argue that most people slide up and down the scale of acting like an amateur or a professional.

One of the most important observations I have made over the past 40 years is that the default is a drift towards being amateur, whereas there needs to be conscious and consistent effort to move towards being professional.

It's a lot like a garden; do nothing and the natural order is for the weeds to invade. Only positive action will keep it looking great and blossoming.

Your business will also need constant attention to ensure it blossoms to its full potential and professional follow-ups are a key component.

I believe professional prospecting and follow-ups are a lot like climbing a mountain:

It's got a base camp where you can prepare and get your kit in order. It has a challenging ascent, where great teamwork will be needed.

Awaiting those who show the real commitment, who have done the preparations, who have invested the effort to get fit for the struggle to make the climb to the summit, is a view of the world that most people will never see.

Our business, your business, can be summed up simply:

"You live a few years like most people won't, so you can live the rest of your life like most people can't"

Following that "climb a mountain theme", here is what I think differentiates amateurs and professionals. Amateurs treat it as a fun hobby and professionals, whether they be full or part-time, treat it as a serious business to transform their future.

Imagine for a moment each and every prospect call you make is like climbing a mountain.

What would the preparations as a leader makes before picking up the phone to call a prospect look like? How would these preparations differ between amateur recruiters and those who are professional in their recruitment.

Amateurs

Before calling, they psych themselves up. They desperately want to get this person to join, so to them it's all or nothing. If they don't get to the summit on this call they have failed. When they discover the prospect is only ready to go to the foothills and not do everything all at once, they experience huge disappointment, coupled with a BIG emotional crash.

The next call is even worse as urgency to recruit is magnified by the pain of the recent total failure. The outcome is the same and the emotional fall is even greater, now their mental resilience "parachute" that can bring them safely down as they fall into despair only works three or four times in quick succession. Then splat their brain takeover and says "not doing any more of this, total waste of time and energy."

So, they stop prospecting, they provide a load of excuses to themselves and others. They stop following up, their personal business stagnates, their team stagnate, their team quit and finally, they quit.

All this drama, and indeed trauma could so easily have been avoided if they had adopted a different mind-set – the mind-set of the true professional.

Professionals

Before each call, they limit their expectation to the simple, single objective of delivering the next step in the process professionally.

There is never a big crash as they are always in control of a professional delivery. They always have a successful call, even when the call ends with an "it's not for me," because to them, they have completed their task. It's time to celebrate their achievement.

As a result of this celebration their brain want's that success rush again, so, bang, they are already dialling the next prospect, with the identical objective of once again delivering the next step professionally. And over time by repeating this process, BOOM, they have a huge business.

In summary

If we think of building a business along the lines of climbing a mountain:

Amateurs, in order to satisfy their personal needs, try to rush prospects straight to the summit of mount Everest with no preparation (they are even wearing flip-flops for heaven's sake), no trail planning, no equipment, no thermals, no sherpas, no oxygen and not even a rescue plan.

Is it any wonder that both they and their prospects crash and burn, with no possibility of future collaborative work.

Professionals, know the Himalayas, they have studied the mountains, they have analysed the past attempts, both theirs and others, learning from the failure and building on the success.

They greet their prospect in the foothills and check how well prepared they are. They ask "are they ready for this? Is this something they really want to do?"

They guide the prospect to basecamp, fully accepting that some choose to leave at this point as it wasn't as they thought it would be. However, those who are left, said they would happily try again in the future maybe under different circumstances.

All the time the professional kept up-skilling their prospect and a few made it to the "just before summit" camp. Again, some left, they were not motivated enough for the ultimate push, but absolutely loved being part of the team and can't wait to join the next expedition.

The final act was to mentor those special few to achieve the peak – their desires finally being meet.

A professional then shares these stories on his blog, in the newspaper and sends postcards. Many of the "silent" onlookers (and passive social media stalkers), who have, up until now been simmering, suddenly decided it is the right time for them put on their climbing pants and make a start.

Professionals create a magical, virtuous circle, where once ignited, success breeds further success.

The route to mastering the follow-up process is clear and simple - "Develop a mind-set that means you want to be professional, to be helpful and patient as you guide people, without expectation towards clarity and confidence in you and the opportunity you are promoting."

Follow-ups offer the potential of true freedom. They are the only way to create a meaningful residual income. The ability to have a recurring income stream coupled with the option of time freedom to enjoy it.

Such a prize must be challenging to obtain. You must have to struggle to create the value of sales that enables your company to pay your income. Let's be honest if it were not difficult, it would be some kind of scam? So, my final thought in this section is aimed at keeping you "honest," not with me but with you, as it is only you who can police this part of your personal mindset!

Bonus time, here are ten ways to build respect and professionalism, not just with prospects but with everyone you come into contact within life.

None of them require natural talent, just a consistent effort to be the best you can.

1. **Being on Time** – Punctuality reflects respect for others and sets a positive tone.

2. **Active Listening** – Fully focusing on what others are saying shows you value their perspective.

3. **Following Through** – Doing what you say you'll do.

4. **Polite Communication** – Speaking with respect, even under stress, keeps relationships strong.

5. **Maintaining a Positive Attitude** – Choosing optimism fosters a better environment for everyone.

6. **Being Prepared** – Taking time to prepare demonstrates respect for others' time and effort.

7. **Taking Responsibility** – Admitting mistakes without excuses shows integrity and maturity.

8. **Showing Gratitude** – Acknowledging others' help or contributions builds goodwill and connection.

9. **Offering help without being asked** – Stepping to assist shows initiative and care for others.

10. **Consistency** – Being dependable in your actions reinforces trust and professionalism.

Chapter 6: Creating a Follow-Up System

"A successful system constantly transforms the efforts of the unskilled into great results"- Howard Philpott

Why is a system so important?

Take a moment to study the illustration above. It is an adaptation of an illustration, from a book by Adam Grant called "Hidden Potential."

It clearly shows why a system is so critical. It is the only way to help many "ordinary people achieve extraordinary results."

Please take a bit of advice, go read the book it's packed full of nuggets that will be just brilliant for your business

Everyone wants great quality people in their team. You know the ones, they are ambitious, independent and just go off like a rocket.

However, if you want those people you need to understand that you must find great quality leads.

Now would be a great time to discuss duplication in our industry. It is the most powerful way to grow your business exponentially. If you have a great system and you get your team to follow you and duplicate using it, promoting it, and teaching that successful system – your business will explode.

In contrast, if you and your team fail to unify around one system coherently, every new team member will hear lots of conflicting views which will ensure that they do nothing for fear of doing the wrong thing.

To illustrate how critical a duplicatable system is, consider these two questions:

Q: Does McDonalds produce the best quality burgers in the world? **A:** In my humble opinion, they do not.

Q: Does McDonalds have the best system to make money from burgers in the world? **A:** Most definitely YES!

Having a successful system that you can just present to new starters is vital.

In today's multi-media world where people are bombarded with messages, ads, posts, not to mention the millions of TV, YouTube, Cable and Satellite channels pumping out thousands of videos a second. How much "head space" does a new recruit have?

You must have a clear system that they can use and share immediately. Do not just give them a blank sheet of paper and expect them, with next to no knowledge or experience to fashion a successful system from scratch.

Returning to McDonalds, no matter how successful you have been, no matter what qualifications you have, when you start a franchise you follow their system.

Put bluntly, if the manual says flip the burger after 1 minute and 47 seconds, you do just that – They don't care about your fancy PhD in hamburger technology, you duplicate the system.

Hopefully you see the importance of a simple, duplicatable system. If you are still in denial, here is another way to look at it. Your recruitment and follow-up system allow a "chicken factory worker" in upstate New York to successfully recruit and start a "cardiovascular surgeon" in Florida?

If you don't have a system you are compelling every generation to make the same mistakes over and over again, as they cannot incorporate refinements into a system that does not exist.

Can you imagine where mankind would be if every new generation did not benefit from the knowledge, wisdom and real-life experiences of their forefathers? The most basic things we take for granted would be lost. OMG each generation would need to re-invent the wheel!

Now you understand how vital a duplicatable system is to your future, let's return to leads or prospects whichever term you prefer, as in this book they are the same

We agreed everyone is looking for great people to join them, so we have the obvious question. "How do I find **GREAT** quality leads?" I hear you ask.

Again, this question drives people deep underground to explore various rabbit holes, when the answer is staring them in the face.

Jim Rohn put it perfectly "success is a refined study of the obvious" and so is the solution to finding great people, and like most important things in life it's blindingly simple. To find great quality leads you first must find a great QUANTITY of leads.

To put it in its most basic term, **a lead is someone** who has signalled they are interested to some degree or other in EXPLORING your opportunity.

ABSOLUTELY EVERYTHING IS
DOWNSTREAM OF LEAD GENERATION

There is a really important mindset adjustment that needs to happen at this point in your business if you are to get the success you so richly desire.

Up until now you have had the act of "sign up" as the barometer of your lead generating success. This has been the destination or end point of your recruitment process.

This needs to change as it has one fundamental and fatal flaw. **You are not in control!**

You must bring your measure of system success within your control. This will completely transform the way you feel about your business. It will transform the way you view the success of your efforts.

The simple change I urge you to make is this - measure and track the number of prospects you generate not the number of sign-ups you make in a week or a month.

The aim is to get the contact details of someone who has "put their hand up" to signal interest – they have not signed a legally binding contract to join, but they have done something, some positive action that signals "hey, I'm curious."

These contact details will, over time, become the <u>most valuable asset</u> your future success will ever own.

Protect them, guard them and above all use them to continually check in with your prospects to see if their time to start is now?

Your prospect file should be so important it becomes one of the things you run back into a burning building for! – Please, the last sentence is purely poetic license, no one should ever return to a burning building (that disclaimer was to satisfy the lawyers).

The systems aim is to provide people with valuable insights and enrichment even if they choose now is not the time for them to start their side hustle with you.

We constantly demonstrate that we will be there to train, to provide practice, rehearsals with constructive criticism. We will be the person in their lives that helps them turn theoretical knowledge into practical and actionable steps.

A system allows for a data driven approach to simplification. Life is so complex. If we do not simplify things we will just hit overload.

Remember the saying "perfect is the enemy of great" so be comfortable with the fact that as we simplify things and look to create groups or "little boxes" to put our prospects into so we can segment them, we will mislabel some.

However, I absolutely guarantee you that the losses from mislabelling errors will be irrelevant when compared to the complete failure caused by quitting due to mental overload.

From experience we are checking to see which one of three categories or boxes our prospect falls into

1. **Not ready now**
2. **A hobbyist**
3. **A part or full time professional**

This grouping will not be a permanent label. People can ebb and flow between them as their life ebbs and flows. This is why you should take very little time in assessing which group to pop a prospect into.

I think Malcolm Gladwell's book "Outliers" would be great here in confirming my hunch of 'don't analyse just go with your gut feeling right now and change later if you feel it's appropriate.'

The reason this segmentation is really important, is because we want to take our prospect on a journey from where they are now to where they'd like to be in the near future, not where they'd like to be in ten years, as they probably have no idea where that would be.

Our system identifies in broad strokes what time availability and attitude towards effort they have right now.

For most people being asked what they'd like in ten years' time is a difficult and painful experience. If you doubt that, think about the last time you went out with a group of people for a meal. How difficult did someone in your party find it to choose their three courses! Think about that these people, capable bright people who couldn't choose their next meal with ease, they have and will choose thousands and thousands of meals in their lives, how could you realistically expect them to choose what they'd like to have or be in a decades time.

How to prospect

This is not a book about how to generate prospects. It's focus is about how to create a system to maximise them over the short and long term.

However, it would be remiss of me not to include a list of the most common prospect generating activities.

Please note, and this is key: You should really speak with your upline as you are much better off copying your teams successful activities – yes it's all about duplication!

All these activities have the aim of gathering contact details of those who express interest, engagement or curiosity in your products or opportunity.

Warm Market Prospecting - Reach out to friends, family, and acquaintances. Use your personal network as a starting point and use the 3rd party approach.

Cold Market Prospecting - Approach people you don't know, such as in public places or online communities. Use leafleting in high-traffic areas to spark interest and gather contact details.

Social Media Marketing - Use platforms like Facebook, Instagram, TikTok, and LinkedIn to share success stories, product testimonials, and lifestyle posts. Engage with followers and people who comment through DMs and public replies, adding these to your prospect list.

Referrals - Ask satisfied customers or team members for recommendations. Offer incentives for referrals.

Networking Events - Attend business meetups, trade shows, and local community events. Exchange contact information and agree to share useful business tips and articles.

Hosting Events - Organise product demonstrations, home parties, or webinars. Provide value and showcase the benefits of your products and business opportunity.

Content Marketing - Create valuable content such as blogs, videos, or podcasts on topics related to your niche. Position yourself as an expert to attract prospects.

Lead Magnets - Offer free resources like e-books, checklists, or webinars in exchange for contact information. Use these leads for follow-up and nurturing.

Personal Branding - Establish a strong personal brand that reflects your values and expertise. Consistently share your story and your journey to attract like-minded prospects.

Paid Advertising - Use Facebook Ads, Google Ads, or Instagram Ads to target specific demographics. Drive traffic to your website or landing pages. Always seek advice before committing to any costs.

Join Communities - Participate in Facebook Groups, forums, or other online spaces related to your niche. Build genuine connections and share helpful insights. Remember there are real world equivalents.

The 3-Foot Rule - Talk to anyone who comes within three feet of you, whether in line, at the gym, or in other casual settings. Treat every interaction as a potential opportunity. Personal note, my boys tell me I need to enter the modern world and change the title of this activity to the "1 metre rule".

How many prospects should you seek to generate?
You'd think this would be as difficult a question to answer as the "How long is a piece of string" question but it is actually unbelievably simple to answer accurately, correctly and more importantly specifically!

Generate 30-50 leads <u>EVERY</u> week using a mix of activities.

Let me explain some fundamental principles in my answer:

1) There is a statistical degree of certainty when you have a reasonable sample size, 30 – 50 prospects a week will deliver the average over time.

   There is safety in numbers and the law of averages so the real risk is just doing a few, go all in and enjoy the increased security that your business will have.

2) By using a mix of many different types of lead generating activities you are, once again spreading the risk. Often when online is slow, the real-world activities deliver great results and vice versa.

3) When you mix many different forms of activities you inevitably discover a mix of prospects, for example door-to-door leafleting could get young or old prospects. This again reduce risk and provides diversity.

This simple and definitive solution provides much needed clarity and direction whether you are yet to start a side hustle or have been involved for decades, this 30 – 50 a week rule provides a fantastic anchor for building a great business.

Chapter 7: The Process of a Great Call

"A great call is no accident"

The best stand-up comedians put hours and hours into rehearsing their jokes so that when the moment comes to perform on stage, you, as a member of the audience feel like it's spontaneous and directed solely at you.

Remember, this fact as you fight your preconceived ideas about being rehearsed and scripted that you will come across in this chapter.

The first seven days after a prospect makes an enquiry are absolutely critical — it's when curiosity is at its peak, when excitement is fresh, and questions are waiting to be answered. It's your window of opportunity to connect while the interest is alive, to build trust and momentum before hesitation or distractions creep in. Waiting too long to reach out sends an unintended message: their interest wasn't a priority to you. In those first seven days, you're not just following up; you're showing them they matter and setting the tone for a potential relationship that could transform both their future and yours.

Train, practice and rehearse with constructive criticism
"Theoretical knowledge is not of much use"

Success in this area is both critical and must be long term. Let's be clear about something here, working for the long term does not mean you have to go at things slowly. You can massively accelerate your growth by doing more, today.

True exponential growth is the compound effort of massive effort multiped by the time over which that effort is maintained, multiplied again by the level of consistent duplication you have in your team.

This process is a marathon, but no one is stopping you from running it at a sprinters pace.

We will cover the full and detailed plan of the process in chapter 13, but here I want to focus on the first few conversations, the ones on which everything else rests.

These will set the scene for every prospect, they will enable those who are keen as mustard to get going now, it will enable you to bring the vision of a new and exciting future to others.

It will also be the gateway conversation that channels prospects into your "prospect pot" where you can keep them simmering until the moment is right for them to join at some time in the near or distant future.

I have seen many systems, some expressly designed for Network Marketing, some are so complicated astrophysicists would struggle. The best one in my opinion, is a Sales Method promoted by Dent Marketing. I really like its combination of simplicity, flexibility and focus.

I love to think of this process as creating the stage to host a great theatre production. The process takes care of all the "stuff" you need to make it truly inspirational; it not only provides the scenery, the lighting, the sound system, it also provides the script, along with the direction.

You just need to complete the task of learning your lines and practising until you get it right.

The combination of a well written script coupled with the professional delivery, set amongst a beautifully lit stage will get rave reviews from your prospects.

Here's the key to why you must follow this process, unless your current process is delivering everything you and your team are seeking when it comes to recruiting superstars.

Have you ever started to watch a film, great cast, it looks fantastic, but when you sit down with your popcorn to watch it, you find after fifteen minutes, you're fidgeting. It just hasn't gripped you, sound familiar?

The start needs to be strong and interesting.

It's the same when it comes to follow-ups, the initial contact needs to be focused and compelling. It is for this reason you follow a process as it ensures you stay on track and offer your prospect the best possible initial information and help.

Below is a visual representation, take a moment to study it, then we can talk through the various stages – Trust me, if you invest the time to professionally practise this, the return on your investment will be enormous, both in your personal effectiveness and in your ability to help your team who struggle with recruitment.

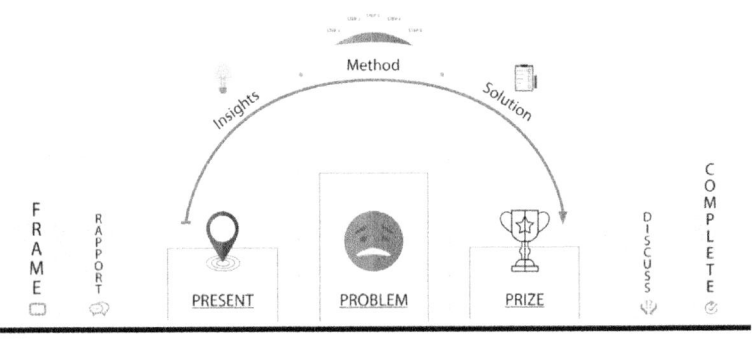

I feel I need to explain one slight shift we need to consider before getting into the detail. Even though we do not "sell" our opportunity, it is vital we take prospects on a journey, so they are ready to "buy" into us, buy into our opportunity, buy into our team and most importantly, buy into our vision of their future, working in partnership with us and our business.

The conversation and the opportunity must be positioned to suit your prospects needs – **do not** exaggerate and **do not** mislead, that would be totally unprofessional and very short sighted.

However, you certainly should use your knowledge and skill to showcase the most appropriate benefits for your prospect.

The transition from one phase to the next should be seamless, it should not feel forced. As you move from Rapport to Present Situation, there is no reason the prospect should know that a shift is happening to your prospect it must flow naturally.

To help me with this concept, I visualise a pulsing dance floor in a club, where a skilled DJ eases from one track to the next keeping the whole dancefloor in step with his transition. This image is in stark contrast to some events I've been to where there is an abrupt change and most of the dancefloor just walks off to the bar.

This adapted version of the Dent Marketing Sales Method is designed to effectively guide conversations when promoting an income opportunity to a prospect. Each phase focuses on helping the prospect see the value of the opportunity in addressing their needs and goals.

It is best to think of this as a skeleton for you to flesh out with your words and phrases that are authentic to you.

Frame
Purpose: Set the tone for an open and focused conversation.
Explanation: Let the prospect know the purpose of the conversation: to explore whether this opportunity aligns with their goals.

Instructions: Start with appreciation: "Thanks for chatting with me today."

Set expectations: "I'd love to learn more about you, share some information about our income opportunity, and see if it's something that might work for you."

Confirm agreement: "Does that sound okay?"

Rapport

Purpose: Build trust and connection.

Explanation: Make the prospect feel comfortable by showing genuine interest in their life.

Instructions: Ask open-ended questions: "What's been keeping you busy lately?" or "What are you most excited about right now?" Share a little about yourself or your experience with the opportunity. Find common ground to build a genuine connection.

Present Situation

Purpose: Understand their current lifestyle, challenges, and goals.

Explanation: Explore their situation to uncover areas where the income opportunity could help.

Instructions: Ask questions like: "How do you feel about your current income and lifestyle?" or "Do you feel like you have enough time and flexibility in your day?" Listen carefully for pain points (e.g., financial stress, lack of flexibility, desire for something more fulfilling). Note any areas where they might want change or improvement.

The Problem

Purpose: Highlight the gap between their current situations and their desired lifestyle.

Explanation: Help them recognise the challenges or limitations they face.

Instructions: Ask, "What would you change about your current situation if you could?" or "What's stopping you from achieving the lifestyle you want?" Reflect back what they share to validate their feelings: "It sounds like you're looking for more [time/freedom/security]." Explore the emotional impact of these challenges.

The Prize

Purpose: Define their dream lifestyle and the benefits they hope to achieve.

Explanation: Shift the conversation to their aspirations and what success means to them.

Instructions: Ask, "If you could design your ideal life, what would it look like?" or "What would having an extra income allow you to do?" Help them visualize the outcome: "Imagine being able to [travel more/spend more time with family/build financial security]." Reinforce the emotional rewards of achieving their goals.

Insights

Purpose: Provide value by offering new perspectives or strategies for achieving their goals.

Explanation: Share insights about how others in similar situations have achieved success through the opportunity.

Instructions: Mention trends or stories: "Many people I've worked with felt stuck like you but found this opportunity gave them [flexibility/freedom]." Share personal or third-party success stories to inspire: "One person I know started with just a few hours a week and now [has achieved X]." Highlight the potential without overpromising.

Method - Our System, this is how our team does things
Purpose: Introduce your system for building a successful income stream.
Explanation: Demonstrate that success is achievable through a clear and supportive process.
Instructions: Explain the system: "We work with a proven approach where you can start part-time and build at your own pace." Break it down into simple steps: "Step 1: Learn the basics. Step 2: Start sharing. Step 3: Build consistently."
Emphasize support: "We have tools, training, and mentorship to guide you every step of the way."

Solution
Purpose: Present the income opportunity as the tailored solution to their needs.
Explanation: Position the opportunity as the bridge between their current situation and their desired lifestyle.
Instructions: Link it to their goals: "Based on what you've shared, this could help you [spend more time with your family/start saving for a home/achieve X goal]."
Share specifics: "You can get started with minimal risk, and we'll set clear steps to get you going."

Make it approachable: "This works for people with busy schedules, and you can scale it as you grow."

Discussion
Purpose: Address questions or concerns and ensure they feel confident.
Explanation: Create space for a two-way dialogue to address hesitations, actively encourage discussion of potential issues.
Instructions: Ask, "What questions do you have so far?" or "Does this sound like something that could fit into your life?" Handle objections with empathy: "I understand; a lot of people feel that way at first. Here's what I've found…" Clarify next steps based on their level of interest: "Would you like to explore this further or think it over?"

Complete
Purpose: Secure commitment or schedule a follow-up.
Explanation: Wrap up with clear next steps to maintain momentum.
Instructions: Depending on where they are in their decision-making process:

> *If they're ready:* "Let's get started with the admin. It will only take a few minutes, I'll guide you through it, then we can get you set up to earn as you learn"

> *If they're unsure:* "Why don't we schedule a follow-up chat in a couple of days after you've had time to think?"

End positively: "I'm here to help you every step of the way, and I'm excited about what this could do for you."

In general attempt to:

- Keep the tone aspirational and empowering. Focus on how the opportunity can change their life in small ways tomorrow and in huge, fundamental ways in the long term.
- Use relatable success stories to inspire belief in what's possible, **for them**.
- Avoid overwhelming them with too much detail upfront — keep it simple and achievable.
- Respect their pace and decisions, offering encouragement without pressure.

This approach ensures the prospect feels understood, inspired, and supported as they explore the income opportunity. This is so simple but seems to be a real thorny issue for most people who are struggling to recruit. They manage to make it the biggest obstacle to moving forward at the right pace, and again, to repeat, it is so simple.

It is just a single call to action, not a multiple choice set of options. It is a single "next step" chosen by you as a result of the information you have gained during this and previous contact.

It could be "the next step is to watch the opportunity presentation; it's about 30 minutes long and packed with useful tips – When do you think you could watch it?" or it might be more like "all that's left is to complete the company admin, it takes about 3 minutes, would now be a good time?"

The aim here is to just continue helping those who are genuinely looking to change their future fortunes to keep progressing towards their stated prize. These tiny little steps are using micro commitments to progress to the stage where they are ready to fully commit to building a big business.

Filling in the company admin to get started is NOT your goal. Obviously, it's a necessary step, but it is just that, another step. The aim of professional follow-ups is to move someone to be a successful member of your team.

A completed form is only the beginning; without action, it's just empty ink on paper, carrying no weight, no change, and no meaning.

This point is so critical. If you fixate on the mere act of completing a joining form, your focus is completely on the wrong measure of success or progress for your business. Notice how judgemental that statement was? Trust me, it needs to be, this as this is a non-negotiable part of building a long-term lifestyle businesses.

Successful team members mean everything, completed joining forms are meaningless without further actions. If they only complete a form, they, you and your company make no sales, so no new customers. Absolutely no one gains anything when the process comes to an end with a successfully completed joining form.

What's THEIR prize?

DO NOT ASSUME you know what your prospect is seeking as their prize in this opportunity. There is a real danger that you become so obsessed with getting someone to join, you lose sight of whether your opportunity is genuinely a good fit for them.

How would they measure success?

A man in his early sixties, expresses an interest in your opportunity, it sounds like he has been quite successful as a civil servant, so you pitch all about retirement, the residual income, the opportunity to enjoy passive income whilst on the beaches of the world.

Only to discover, when you have already painted this wildly vivid picture, that this horrifies him and is the exact opposite of what he was looking for.

If you had checked professionally, you would have discovered he was looking for a side hustle to build, in his spare-time over the next few years.

So that when it does come to enforced retirement from his job, his now blossoming side-hustle can take its place as his full-time activity, because the very last thing he wants to do is to retire and in his words "Wait to die."

Make sure you are absolutely certain of what your prospect wants as their "prize."

If you fail to take the time needed to work this out in detail, you are building a business relationship built on sand, as there is no firm foundation.

Chapter 8: Tools for Effective Follow-Up

"These tools magnify effort the more you use them."

Over the years, I have been observing true professionals who have collectively made in excess of 500,000 follow-ups, and I have noticed a pattern in their finely tuned approach.

They have a "tool kit" that does much of the heavy lifting when it comes to actually setting the scene, which enables prospects to visualise being successful by joining them and their opportunity.

In our profession a "toolkit" comprises different types of what could loosely be described as marketing assets. They are both physical and digital.

Their purpose is to help a prospect read or watch things about our opportunity to re-enforce what we have said.

Now many of these seasoned professionals have refined their tool kit over the years, to more reflect their personal preferences, but all of them have the same basic kit with some new (twenty-first century) additions.

Why have a tool kit?

As you start making follow-ups you will soon realise it helps to have assistance in painting a great picture of a bright future.

We humans are great story tellers, we think in stories and emotions, we do not think in spreadsheets and formulas.

Your tool kit helps with great storytelling, it improves both your efficiency and effectiveness. As an illustration, you are speaking to someone who is interested in understanding the detail of your business model and the different ways they could earn with your opportunity.

Now you could spend 40 minutes running through the business presentation, or you could simply dip into your toolbox and grab the business presentation video and say, "I will send over a video, that clearly explains all about the various income streams. You'll be able to pause and rewind to make sure you fully understand. It's about the length of an episode of a TV soap, but with a real-world life changing story line."

Whatever you say, you should finish, by asking the most important question, "when will you sit down to watch it, as I'd really like to chat once you have."

When you step back and think about it, creating your own personal tool kit is completely in line with the philosophy of Network Marketing. Do the work once and get paid over and over again. Record the presentation once and use it over and over and over again.

Create an "interview" leaflet once and send it over and over and over again.

Like all occupations, it's acceptable to borrow tools from others when you start but over time you are going to discover you must make your own, particularly your story.

If you don't how can you expect others to do it? And that is the $64,000 question – how can you expect others to do something you don't? This is where duplication dies and businesses never gain their true potential.

This is a basic list of the tools or assets that will be most useful.

1. Your personal story
2. Other people's stories
3. Team success
4. Newspaper
5. Business presentation
6. Online weekly workshop

This "toolbox" principle is the key to our industry's success.

We seek to inspire people and build assets that require big upfront effort, in the expectation that this will create an income stream that requires minimal effort into the future. These tools will help you achieve success this much quicker.

1. Your personal story

Let's dive straight into the personal story. Straight away I need to correct a myth that has somehow sprung up in recent decades, that's the "my story is boring" myth. It tends to be twinned with another, the "no one is interested" myth.

I can tell you with certainty; your story is both interesting and exciting to millions of other people. Whatever you have achieved I know there are millions who would love to accomplish the same. At its most basic the success you have achieved just by starting is outside the comfort zone of millions and millions. The fact that you have made sales and earned an additional family income is almost superhuman to the tens of millions of people who are convinced they could not sell anything.

And don't get me started on how amazing you look now you have started to build a residual income, an income that for almost all is beyond their wildest dreams. So don't you ever tell me your story is either boring or not of interest – as you would be wrong, just plain wrong.

Now you would be right if you were to say "How can I make my story clearer or more inspiring, whilst maintaining its authenticity."

This is actually quite a challenge to accomplish well on your own. My advice here is to buddy up with someone who would also like to improve their personal story. You can then take it in turns to quiz each other about your achievements, the small early ones are often much more powerful as these are more realistic to prospects. Then write a "newspaper article" about your buddy's story.

I would over a short period seek to do this exercise with a few different people; one of whom should be someone who you hold in high esteem.

You now have a number of draft story options, take the best from them all and fashion a story that is authentically you in both fact and spirit. If you are fun and cheeky that should be present in your story, but always truly professional.

Once you have the final version, cut out half the words or have ChatGPT do this bit for you, by popping in your full version and ask for it to be cut to about a five-minute read.

When you have done this, go out and buy yourself a small reward and place it on your desk but do not open it yet. By getting to this stage with your personal story you have just accomplished one of the most fundamental foundations of building a successful MLM business.

However, there are a few things to complete before you get to enjoy your reward. I just wanted you to have the extra motivation of being able to constantly see your reward as you settle down to truly master the art of the personal story.

Over the next FEW days, not as long as a week, I want you to do two things with your story.

- Use it as a "screenplay script" and create a video of you telling your story. A great tip here is to have a couple of photos you can hold up to help with the visuals.

- Create a single page "interview with" leaflet (see below). A great tip for this is to have some professional style photos taken (doesn't need to be done by a professional but needs to look professional – Google can help you with this).

You now have your story in many formats, that you can deliver it professionally in person, you can send a video, and you can post the leaflet.

How impressed would a prospect be if they received something as stunning as this. It is so easy to produce. Use the questions as a template and insert your own answers, it looks even better in glorious colour.

This upfront effort will pay you back massively, not only in your follow-ups but also the leveraged growth that will come from your team following you.

Before we move on to the next item in our toolbox list, and you enjoying your reward, I want you to consider this:

Integrity Moment: There is a significant risk to your future success right now, and you probably have no idea that it's about to wreck your otherwise bright future.

You, yes, I mean you – while you are reading this, (as you chat to yourself, in your head) saying that sounds brilliant, I must record that – and then doom strikes, you use the "L" word. I am sure you know we humans are wired for instant gratification. We want to see progress now, rewards now. Tasks without an immediate payoff get pushed to "later".

Later, is a dangerous place where intentions go to die.

This desire to procrastinate is hardwired into our DNA, its pervasive and needs constant attention, or it spreads into everything that you value. Some tasks may seem unnecessary in the moment, but their value becomes crystal clear down the line.

Think of a chef sharpening their knife. It's not flashy or exciting—it doesn't create a meal, nor does it fill a plate. But when the heat is on and orders are flying in, that sharp knife becomes the difference between chaos and excellence.

Or consider a teacher preparing a FAQs sheet for students. It's easy to skip, especially when the immediate priority is lesson planning or marking papers. But when students are armed with clear answers and fewer repetitive questions arise, both teaching and learning become smoother.

These are the kinds of tasks that make future moments better, easier, or more productive. Yet, because the benefits aren't immediate, they're often the first to get delayed or dismissed.

The secret is to view these tasks as investments. They don't demand much time or effort today, but their payoff is exponential. A few minutes spent sharpening a tool, preparing a resource, or organising your thoughts can save hours of stress or inefficiency in the future.

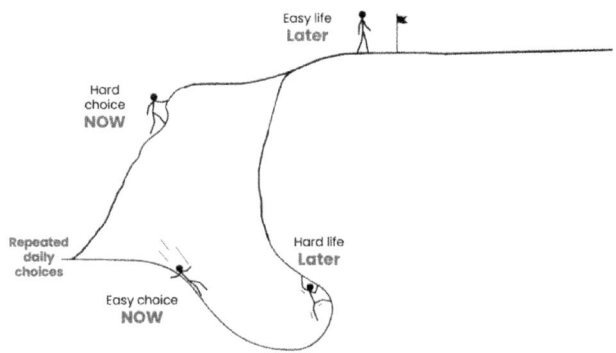

When you approach tasks with this mindset, you're not just working for today — you're building a better tomorrow. And when that tomorrow arrives, you'll thank yourself for having the foresight to prepare. After all, the future is shaped by the choices we make today, one sharpened knife or well-crafted FAQ at a time.

For us it's not going to be a kitchen knife, but it could be an FAQs sheet with the most common questions prospects are likely to ask.

Adopt the philosophy, that prioritises effort into tasks that will provide repeated benefit over those activities that will be one hit wonders that have no future income enabling properties.

2. Other people's stories

When you are following up prospects, the vast, overwhelming majority, in fact I think it would be more appropriate to say all of your prospects are only interested in getting the answers to three basic questions:

1. **Can I trust you?**
2. **Can I do it?**
3. **Is it worth it for me?**

That's it, genuinely that is it. Now this simplicity hides the full complexity of human nature, this is why other peoples stories are so important. They enable us with integrity and authenticity to help prospects evaluate the 2nd and 3rd questions:

For the, "**Can I do it question?**" we play a mental game of snap, as we are looking for a story that matches the prospects current situation, a story that is true and uplifting, one that could be backed up with a meeting or conversation.

If your prospect was a mum of two young children, as you are chatting, she is subconsciously asking herself "sounds great but you can't do it if you've got the kids, don't be foolish and think you can". Prospects subconscious minds are usually in pessimistic mode when talking to a relative stranger about business.

The answer to offset this incorrect assumption on your prospect's part is to use other people's stories, so if this were me, I'd dive into my library of stories and pull out, a suitable one that enables me to shout "SNAP" in my mind, not to my prospect, obviously.

Here's an example: "My friend Vicky has been building this business for about 4 years now. She has two wonderful little kids, Seb and Grace, they are her world. In fact, she tells everyone they are the very reason she is building this business. It enables her to provide them with the lifestyle, they deserve – they get the trips to Disneyland, and they get a mum that has the flexibility to be there for sports days. The £3,000 - £4,000 a month income makes a huge difference to the family budget, enabling treats."

Then I'd follow-up with "would that be the kind of side-hustle income and lifestyle you'd like to explore?"

Other people's stories are like an unlimited supply of the "get out of jail free" cards in Monopoly, but here in the real world you can play them any time you feel you are in a jam. It's like having an army of people ready and willing to help you treat any incorrect assumption on the part of your prospect.

Important note: The reason it is vital to get as much detail as you can on your prospect's current situation, is to help you identify which is the best story to use, and here's another tip – there is no rule that says you can only play one at a time, it is really good to "tag team" stories to maximise their effect.

Amateur v Professional
Amateurs, sort of remember stories: "A women I saw had some kids and I think she's doing ok – So you can do it"

Professionals, make it their mission to harvest stories, they understand the role they play and they practice when to use them. Jim Rohn has a great quote for why you should ensure you know the full story. "The drama is in the detail."

These small details add colour and emotional reality to what could otherwise be a bland story.

I can tell you professionals rehearse this key skill.

I was talking with a truly successful couple about the importance of other people's stories and the wife (no names to protect the innocent) said "it still makes me laugh, even after thirty odd years of observing it, we will be driving along the freeway, and I look over to my husband, who is driving, and I can see his lips moving, I can actually see he is having a conversation with some imaginary prospect in his head. Sometimes, when I'm feeling a bit mischievous, I butt in and join the conversation. What's the issue? Once he responded with, I was sharing Joan's story that highlights how people with anxiety can succeed at a pace that matches their day-to-day emotional state so there's never any external pressure, you do what you can, when you can."

Professionals make it look easy in the moment, because they have done the hard work previously.

Another area where other peoples' stories can be really useful, is to showcase different income levels. Now your story is always the most powerful, even when the income is small (everyone will have a different definition of small). You can use other people's stories to illustrate that much larger incomes are possible with the right mix of effort, consistency and time.

Again, I must be clear, you should never feel your story is inadequate when compared to others. Everyone moves at different speeds due to different circumstances and desires.

If you struggle to be proud of your story, ask yourself "Am I happy with the choices and effort I am putting in"? If you are happy with the activity levels then you need to accept your story genuinely reflects what you seek to achieve.

If you are not happy with your choices and effort levels – the answer is blindingly obvious, change your choices and up your activity for the next 90 days.

Once you finish your personal story, your next goal is to encourage your team to create theirs, starting with a leaflet and a video as the first steps in building their own toolbox.

3. Team Success
This isn't a tool based on a single event or story; it's more of a collection of evidence to show your prospect that they'll have not only your support but also the backing of your entire team community.

Ultimately, it's a tool that demonstrates you are fostering a supportive culture.

It's all about the fact that the team they will belong to, is recognised for being epic, it's a community where people expect to be successful, examples could be:

Achieving incentive trips – This creates a can-do attitude every time the company announces a new one. There is a team wide mind-set, "**we can do this,**" because we have a way of breaking it down into clear targets with the required activities to ensure they are met, and we are successful.

Awards – Make it a team priority to win as many as possible. You and your team should do all you can to create a sense of "We can do this."

If you find you are not excelling at this or there are just no awards to aim for, here is a simple solution to guarantee success. Launch some team wide awards, make them varied so they evenly disperse the recognition throughout your team. You can do this by segmenting them into rank groups and /or time in the business. It is also good team fun, to create some awards that reflect non business areas.

Go on be brave, *bring the joy.*

For this section who do I consider "your team"? – For me, when talking to prospects, your team would obviously start with your downline, it would also include all of your upline's teams.

The reason I have a broad definition of team when talking to the outside world is based o
n the fact that anyone joining you will have the opportunity to gain support from all of your uplines' experience as well as yours.

It is also possible to form great relationships with crosslines to provide mutual support and collaboration.

4. Newspaper

In this digital world, where we have instant news delivered to our smartphones, it's easy to forget that as humans we have been reading the written word for millennia. As of October 2024, there were 2.4 million daily national newspapers in circulation in the UK.

This fact clearly illustrates there is still a massive desire to have information provided in a physical document that you can read through.

A physical brochure, booklet, or newspaper that promotes your opportunity isn't just a luxury — it's an essential tool. Being able to hand or send something tangible to a prospect is a crucial component of your success strategy, providing a more lasting and impactful promotional resource than any digital post.

It also provides you with a tool that can be read and shared with other people. When you speak with as many people as I have over the past 40 years, patterns emerge as to how people become "lucky" in building their business.

Here is one of the more common stories about how people join an opportunity by chance. – "I was visiting my sister, and saw she had a brochure on the kitchen table. Being curious I took a peek and discovered an opportunity that was perfect for me, and as it happens my sister never joined."

If you don't leave prospects with something real and physical that directs them to you and your opportunity you are missing a trick.

What's your opportunity "newspaper"? – If I was a prospect, what would you hand to me, right now that I could take away with me and read when convenient AND leave on my coffee table for others to see?

It is too easy to just have digital tools, because it needs more effort and planning to have something physical. Too many people fool themselves into believing people don't want it these days, let me tell you plainly, they are wrong.

Having a blend of tools for both the digital and physical world is an absolute must, if you want to maximise the effectiveness of your efforts. It's also worth remembering that if you don't have and use everything, your team will duplicate your narrow approach and massively limit the growth potential of the whole team.

If you are an aspiring leader, now is the time to start leading.

You will set the pace that your whole team travels at, they copy what you do, more than what you say, so your goal is to make what you do speak louder than what you say, then people will listen.

5. Business Presentation

I am sure your company has a business presentation. However, in my experience these tend to be over complicated, and way too technical. They often miss how important the personal reasons and emotional feelings are to a prospect when they are deciding, whether to join or not.

Therefore, I think it is vital that you create your own business presentation event. Obviously this needs to be based on the factual details that your company HQ uses, but it needs the personal, emotional and authentic stories that you and your team can use to bring an otherwise dull PowerPoint presentation to life.

The details of the analysis of any particular income structure, commission, bonuses and incentives will always run the risk of being a little dry but they must be accurate and not misleading.

Over the years I have attended and presented opportunity meetings in many different countries. Below is my guide to hosting a fabulous in person opportunity meeting.

What does a Great Opportunity Presentation look like?

Attending a well-executed business opportunity meeting can be a transformative experience for potential team members.

These gatherings provide an invaluable first impression, offering insights into the opportunity, the culture, and the support system available.

To understand what makes such events successful, we've captured feedback from individuals who've attended exceptional meetings in the past.

Their comments highlight the key elements that helped them feel welcomed, informed, and inspired to take the next step.

By focusing on these points, you can create an environment that leaves prospects excited and eager to join your journey.

- The venue and time had been known for a while, so I was able to plan in advance.

- As soon as I entered the hotel foyer, I knew exactly where to go—no awkward moments feeling lost. *"I'm new to this and already way outside my comfort zone."*

- Walking into the room, the atmosphere was buzzing. I was greeted warmly, in a friendly and professional manner. Right away, I felt welcome, and the *"Will I fit in?"* question was answered positively.

- The music struck the perfect balance—not too dull to fade into the background but not so loud that I couldn't hold a conversation.

- As the meeting began, there was a palpable sense of excitement. It wasn't over-the-top, cheerleading energy but a genuine feeling that the future held real potential.

- The opportunity was presented in a **simple**, **concise**, and **compelling** way that made logical sense to me. *"It just clicked."*

- An experienced Team Builder shared her story, and I thought, *"WOW – I never realised you could earn so much from a side hustle."*

- A new team member then spoke about his first three months. Even though he was clearly nervous, he had made over £1,000 in just 90 days. *"If he can do it, maybe I can too."*

- The presentation continued with clear evidence of why **now,** is the best time is to get started in a side hustle.

- The surprise for me was the guy who appeared via video, explaining how he makes money while he sleeps. *"That's the dream – and the best part? He looked and spoke like an ordinary person. Total game-changer."*

- Then I learned it wasn't just about money. There were trips and cars available even for new people. *"That could be me!"* Seeing people living it up in exclusive destinations made me think, *"What do I need to do to be part of that?"*

- After the presentation, there were complimentary teas, coffees, and drinks. What a relief! *"I hate the awkwardness of figuring out who's paying."*

- I decided to join right then—not because it was *"free to try"* but because I wanted change, and these people made me believe I could achieve that with them.

- Following the meeting, there was a brief *"Flying Start"* session. It was informal but packed with practical advice. I could already see that there'd be plenty of support. *"I won't have to figure this out alone."* The 20-minute basic training gave me just enough to get started and avoid some now-obvious pitfalls.

- I left feeling confident that I could succeed by simply inviting others to events like this. It's the perfect way to grow my team while I continue learning.

- Oh, and it wasn't the dull evening I expected. I'm already looking forward to the next one! *"I made a note when they announced the dates for the next three meetings."*

As a side note, any event along these lines would also provide a great "mental boost" for existing team members – both to gain from and contribute to, whether that's by sitting in the audience listening to stories, by being one of the speakers or by being part of the team, manning the registration desk. "Sometimes you need the meeting and sometimes the meeting needs you."

The next step, once you are comfortable having delivered a number of "live in person" events is to take them online.

Let's talk about the difference between live and recorded as some people believe they will have the same impact, and as it is easier just to share a recording, they believe there is little point in doing live events.

Throughout my whole life I have had a fascination for facts and the sciences. I have a genetic aversion to "mumbo jumbo." At university I studied Maths and Statistics. I obviously infected my three boys with this bug as, at university their degree courses were economics, natural sciences and astrophysics.

So please understand my complete unease when I say that there is something "magical" (yes, mumbo jumbo) about doing these events live. I cannot explain it – but there is absolutely no doubt, these events are much, much more successful when done live.

Maybe it's because everyone knows a "LIVE" event always feels more authentic, coupled with the understanding that these people are showing up right now, to provide me with an insight into a potentially bright future.

Or just maybe (I can't believe I am about to say this), maybe it's the universe providing you with much greater rewards for taking the extra effort and finding a greater level of courage to host a live event, rather than just send out recordings.

It is therefore much more effective to do a weekly or monthly "LIVE" business presentation, but it is critical to have a recording of a recent event that you can let prospects watch. This is a vital tool as it enables you to share a professional presentation with an excited prospect.

This recording is a great tool for new people as it allows them to showcase a really professional event while they are still working out which way is up.

To summarise, host regular real life opportunity events – In addition host online events, the same as real world, just done remotely.

As a great secondary tool, record one and use it where a "live" event is too far away, either in terms of geography or time.

Key point to remember: Live events will always be more effective but for some specific purposes a recording will be more efficient.

6. The Weekly Online Training Workshop

We reach the final item on our list of basic tools for prospects, and I know what you are thinking, how can a training workshop be a prospecting tool?

What possible benefit can there be from inviting a prospect to a training workshop?

One of the biggest obstacles to starting a side-hustle is a fear of failure, especially in today's world where social media, dominates our personal interactions.

People are overly concerned with what other people will think, and in today's world what they will post about them.

Even those prospects that outwardly appear confident and successful harbour these doubts.

I guarantee all, yes ALL, every single one of the prospects you generate will at some point ask themselves the question **"Can I do this?"**

In most cases you counteract this often irrational fear by using stories, yours and other peoples, as we have discussed previously. However, there will be many occasions where you will need a different tool to help solve this problem.

This is where a basic level, weekly online workshop can help; the subject matter for these is always generic. It should cover material that would be of value in almost any business or side-hustle, it can even cover topics that are just helpful in life in general.

Here is a list of 26 weekly topics, so stop dithering as that's the next six months taken care of for you:

1. Master Your Mindset
2. Confidence Unlocked
3. Time Management for Busy People
4. Turning Fear into Fuel
5. The Art of Networking
6. Mastering the Balancing Act
7. Goal Setting That Works
8. Personal Branding 101
9. Effective Communication
10. The Power of Persistence
11. The Confidence Gap
12. Problem-Solving Like a Pro
13. Your Inner CEO
14. Vision Boards and Visualisation
15. Stress Less, Achieve More
16. Unlock Your Creativity
17. Developing Emotional Intelligence
18. Influence Without Authority
19. Taking the Leap
20. Building Mental Resilience
21. Creating Positive Habits
22. Overcoming Imposter Syndrome
23. Storytelling for Connections
24. The Power of Active Listening
25. Managing Overwhelm
26. Unlocking Your Potential

By keeping the content general, they will be of great value to anyone, including your prospects.

Like most of the tips in this book they can be multi-purposed. By recording these weekly sessions, you are creating content that can be transformed with very little effort for your YouTube channel or your podcasts.

Then, when someone in your team, or a prospect you are in conversation with has a specific problem say, for example "time management", you can just whizz them the link to your prerecorded, "Time Management for Busy People" video on your YouTube channel and instantly provide help and support.

This is the key to running a huge network business without imploding - do something once, that enables you and your team to keep re-using it many times.

These online weekly workshops can be truly special if you create a culture of showing up throughout your team. Like all new things it will take time and perseverance to get them established, but once you have overcome the initial inertia, they will become a staple of your team's calendar.

Finally, remember the purpose of the weekly workshop is twofold, firstly it's to upskill your current team.

However its primary purpose it to create an attraction, a gravity that will over time pull in the hard working and professional super stars we are all looking to recruit.

Part 3

The Art of Follow-Ups

Chapter 9: Rehearsing for the Ideal Conversation

The following are some great words and phrases – it's time to rehearse and practice.

Let me paint a picture for you of my world right now. As I write this chapter, my music playlist, is currently pulsating "4 My People" by Missy Elliot (Basement Jaxx remix) extremely loudly in my noise cancelling headphones, it's 5:30am on Saturday morning and I'm sat in a motorway service Costa Coffee as it's the only place open.

As I drift into nodding along with the beat, I'm seeking inspiration to illustrate how little effort people actually make in getting better at having great conversations.

I look past my laptop screen and see the twinkling 10 feet tall Christmas tree and the idea just pops into my head. It, like almost all of this book is something I have used many times over the years, so let me paint the scene for you.

Your little "Jonny" who is a shy 6 six-year-old has been chosen to be a shepherd in the school Nativity play. He has one line to say, just a single line of 17 words. My question to you as his doting parent is simple; how long would you spend with little

Jonny rehearsing until he absolutely nailed his one line like an Oscar winning actor?

When I ask this of a live audience at an event, almost instantly and unanimously the room blasts "as long as it takes" – I'm always stunned by the emotional strength that those without children of their own have in their response.

No one in the room thinks that their collective response is important or of any consequence, because to a man and woman they just fail to see it as news.

To them it's so obvious it's akin to not being surprised that the sun will rise again tomorrow.

But to me, it's a revelation and indeed it becomes a revelation to the audience once I draw their attention to a comparison between that response and their response to my next question.

Looking for the same instant, emotional response, I ask the question: How long would you rehearse until you had the responses to the most common queries your prospects might ask?

What a difference, the room always falls silent. People who were only moments ago full of life and energy have suddenly been rendered mute. After some prompting, a few people offer a time frame, but most just sit in stunned silence.

For most people this stark contrast is a shock to them. There is really no hiding place mentally, it is a brutal moment, a shocking piece of unusual clarity in their personal self-awareness.

I continue to press, why is it that you, with huge conviction say "As long as it takes" with Jonny's single line, but it's next to nothing when it comes to shaping a better future?

Then the self-awareness clarity evaporates, and the completely false excuses start. I don't want to dwell on them but here is the gist of the most common one, when it's about little Jonny it's different because I want everything to be good for him.

As a dad I get that, I genuinely do but here is the self-awareness piece I'd like you to take away and reflect on.

Would little Jonny's future be brighter if your future had a significant residual income coupled with time freedom to devote to enjoying those once in a lifetime family moments guilt free.

My opinion is shaped by experience and deeper analysis. Put simply, people see a direct link between the effort of rehearsal with Jonny's line and a successful outcome in the Nativity play.

They do not have the same clarity or faith in the link between investing time in rehearsing their prospect lines and a successful outcome, namely an increase in income and a brighter future for them and little Jonny.

One of the aims of this book is to help you discover that clarity. I was just 19 when I had the privilege of spending quality time with Jim Rohn. For me, my life changing moment was the adoption of two of his pillars of success as my core philosophy for life:

1. "work harder on yourself than you do on your job"

2. "activities are the birth pains of success"

For me, the personal philosophy we choose to live by becomes the benchmark and much of the mental anguish we suffer comes not from the outside world but from within us, when we fail to meet our own standards.

I know that by adopting these two themes as unshakeable beliefs, my world has been far better. My promise to you is this, - "adopt an aspirational philosophy and you will massively stack the odds of success in your favour if you invest time and effort in YOU."

Getting better yourself, is the fundamental foundation on which to build success. It is the way to exponential growth. I know most people doubt this, so I want to really try to explain how the effort you put into improving your skill set will have huge, positive implications for your business and life.

If you get better, your personal results get better. This is something that everyone agrees with on both a logical and emotional level. Let's call this Stage 1 improvement, by definition it affects just you, one person.

Before you say that philosophy is all about business, I'd have to say you are so wrong. Part of my working "work harder on yourself than you do on your job," directs me to actually put time aside to work on being a better husband, father and friend.

Likewise, the "activities are the birth pains of success." Philosophy provides the mental foundation to carve out time in a busy schedule to play rugby with my boys.

When your business philosophy is in conflict with your home philosophy, you experience emotional turmoil. The easy way to avoid this is to have a universal life philosophy that guides you in all walks of life's adventures. There is no difference in the way I conduct myself in business or home.

There can be no greater authenticity then genuinely being you, in all settings and at all times.

Now let me talk to you on the cascading and compounding effects that this, your personal improvement unleashes.

Following your improvement, you now exert a more effective influence over the people you interreact with most often. Your improvement raises the average of your circle of influence. This is Stage 2 – affecting say 20 people.

The cascade continues over time, as you continue to improve. This then, influences those around, who in turn improve and influence those around them. The geometric progression means the 20 that you influence, influence 20 others. That's Stage 3, where the 20 you personally influenced, now influence their 20, which means we now we have 400 people affected.

Stage 4, you continue, they continue, and it just grows, compounding at each stage with you influencing new people who you have only recently meet. The 400 from Stage 3 influence the 20 people in their circle of influence, now we are up to 8,000 in total.

Now I am acutely aware that nothing ever follows with such perfect symmetry, but the path is indisputable.

The effort of your improvement has the potential to deliver a disproportionate business outcome.

Trust me, it is always worth the effort. There are also non-financial reasons; for me one of the most meaningful is the satisfaction I gain from applying my improvements to help others achieve more.

If we return to that nativity scene, is there any doubting the fact that when little Jonny gets to see his parent continuing to learn and work hard to become better, he will absorb this truly valuable life skill.

What's the difference between amateurs and professional when it comes to being prepared?

An amateur practices until they get it right once,
in stark contrast
a professional practices until they get it right <u>always</u>.

Most people feel uncomfortable when they are making follow up calls, so you are not alone. I have great news to share with you. I have a sure-fire way to help you become comfortable with those calls and it's unbelievably simple – just do more of them!

There is really only one more thing I can do to help with this, and in the next chapter I have worked with my friend ChatGPT to organise a range of phrases that will suit different personality types.

Use these as sparks. The aim is not to learn these verbatim but to use them to fashion a line that is you, in your authentic words and tone.

But, before that, I must give you two more general tips, which I really want you to grasp.

One: Do not use insider language on the outside. By this I mean do not use ANY word or term that needs an understanding of your company's pay plan or systems. It will completely alienate your prospect as it will immediately tell them they are an outsider – not one of the group and this feeling of exclusion will be very difficult to shake as you progress through the follow up process.

Two: Avoid politics and religion. I don't care how passionately you hold your views, follow up calls are not the place to share or debate them.

The following chapter has a buffet of phrases for many different types of personalities – mix and match, tweak and shape, until you have embedded your personality in them. Make them your own.

Once you have crafted your ideal script practice it. Practice in the car. Practice it while brushing your teeth (do this silently or it gets messy, I know from experience).

Then the most import part is, go hone your new skill by practising on real prospects – remember you can't say the wrong thing to the right people, so now you can feel satisfied as you "cock it up with confidence. "

Building a business is a "doing" activity so grab your courage and go and do it!

Chapter 10: Starting and Unsticking Conversations

This section is aimed at providing you with a starting point, it is deliberately not meant to be a final script. If I provided you with a finished, final script it would fail, for the simple fact it would not sound or feel like you, it would not be authentic.

The solution is to read through these and see which of them chimes with you, then say them in your words, rewrite them, tweak them and above all else, own them.

Note: This re-write has one important restrictive condition. You cannot make them much longer – That would be you adding in waffle as you lack the confidence to be brief and concise, the point to keep in mind is that this is a business call.

I have sought to cover the most common struggle points when having a conversation:

Opening Line: For so many people this is the one that truly stumps them. I feel it's the number one "**excuse**," so get this one sorted first – and remember, it will always seem new and unique to each prospect as they will have never heard it before.

Transition from Chit-Chat Line: This moves you gracefully from opening rapport building to the substance of the call.

Uncover the Pain Point Line: Help your prospect find the space to articulate their real issue, this one needs you to build in silence – give your prospect time to think and answer, NEVER jump in with your assumptions about their pain point.

Refocus Line: We've all been there—a prospect call starts strong, but then it happens, the energy dips, the conversation drifts, or worse, it stalls completely. In moments like these, knowing how to pivot and refocus is crucial. Here's how you can use personality-specific strategies to keep the conversation flowing and discover what truly matters to your prospect.

Permission to Move Forward: It pays to gain ongoing permission to progress to the next step or phase. These little check ins help your prospect know you are always focused on what's right for them.

I have grouped the possible phrases by personality types, just to give some structure, but you feel free to mix and match. We are all a complex mess of personalities, so blend away – get a script that is true to you.

1. **Friendly and Warm**
2. **Direct and No-Nonsense**
3. **Curious and Engaging**
4. **Empathetic and Relatable**
5. **Playful and Light-hearted**
6. **Professional and Credible**

Then write out your favourite lines and go practice, find prospects and practice, practice and after a while you will see improvements that you can incorporate and accelerate your improvement by, yes more practice – one day in years to come you will wake up and discover you are a "grand master" at follow-ups and even more importantly you have a team of aspiring "grand masters" duplicating your success.

Write your phrases, copy them and place them all over your physical world and your digital world. Go be brave and have fun.

1. Friendly and Warm

Opening Line: "Hi [Prospect's Name], this is [Your Name]. I noticed you recently requested more information about [topic/product]. I'm so glad you reached out! I'd love to answer any questions and share how it could work for you. Do you have a quick moment to chat?"

This line sets a warm and friendly tone, making the prospect feel acknowledged and valued from the start.

Transition from Chit-Chat Line: "I'm really glad we got a chance to connect! Since you reached out for more info, I'd love to share how [topic/product] could make a difference for you. What sparked your interest in this?"

This smoothly bridges casual conversation into the core purpose of the call while inviting the prospect to share their thoughts.

Uncover the Pain Point Line: "I'd love to get a better sense of what you're looking for. What made you decide to reach out about this opportunity? Is there something you're hoping it could help with?"

This line invites the prospect to reflect on their motivations and openly share their needs.

Refocus Line: "Sounds like we've covered a lot! Let me bring it back—what's the one thing you'd really like to get out of this opportunity?"

For someone who thrives on connection and values relationships, this approach is ideal. You're acknowledging the flow of the conversation while gently steering it back to what matters.

Permission to Move Forward: "Does this all sound good? Would you be open to taking the next step, [like attending a meeting or watching a video]?"

2. Direct and No-Nonsense

Opening Line: "Hi [Prospect's Name], this is [Your Name]. I saw that you're interested in learning more about [topic / product]. Let's get straight to it—do you have a couple of minutes to see how it could benefit you?"

This direct approach immediately establishes your respect for their time and your confidence in the opportunity.

Transition from Chit-Chat Line: "Thanks for taking the time to chat. Let's dive right in—I'll quickly walk you through how [topic/product] works and the key benefits. Sound good?" This line signals a quick and efficient transition, ensuring the conversation stays productive.

Uncover the Pain Point Line: "Let me ask you straight— what's the main challenge or goal that made you interested in learning more about this? I want to make sure; we focus on what's most relevant for you."

This straightforward question gets right to the heart of their motivation, showing that you're focused on delivering value.

Refocus Line: "Let's cut to the chase—what's the most important question you need answered to decide if this is right for you?"

For prospects who value efficiency and clarity, don't dance around the subject.

Permission to Move Forward: "Shall we move to the next step, [like attending a meeting or watching a video]?"

3. Curious and Engaging

Opening Line: "Hi [Prospect's Name], this is [Your Name]. I saw you requested more info about [topic/product], which caught my attention. I'm curious—what specifically interested you? Let's explore how it might be a great fit for you!"

This line taps into their curiosity and opens the floor for them to share their initial thoughts.

Transition from Chit-Chat Line: "It's great getting to know you! I'm curious—what's the main thing you're hoping to achieve or solve with [topic/product]? Let's focus on that!"

This keeps the conversation exploratory while guiding it toward meaningful discussion.

Uncover the Pain Point Line: "I'm curious—when you left your details, what was going through your mind? Were you looking to solve a specific problem or explore new possibilities?"

This helps uncover their true motivations by inviting them to reflect on their decision to seek more information.

Refocus Line: "I feel like we've touched on a lot, but I'd love to know—what's the one thing that excites or concerns you most about this?"

For the naturally inquisitive prospect, this line invites them to reflect and share their deeper thoughts.

Permission to Move Forward: "Does this align with what you are looking for? Would you like to take the next step, [like attending a meeting or watching a video]?"

4. Empathetic and Relatable

Opening Line: "Hi [Prospect's Name], this is [Your Name]. I noticed you were interested in [topic/product] and wanted to personally follow up. I've been where you are and found this to be really helpful—do you have a moment to chat about it?"

This line conveys empathy and builds immediate rapport by sharing a relatable experience.

Transition from Chit-Chat Line: "I really appreciate you sharing a bit about yourself. Let's talk about how [topic / product] could fit into your life and make things easier for you. What's most important to you right now?"

This transition ensures the prospect feels heard while moving the conversation toward their goals.

Uncover the Pain Point Line: "I know that everyone has their own story. What's going on in your life right now that made you feel this opportunity might be worth exploring?"

This helps the prospect to open up about their personal challenges or motivations in a way that feels natural and supportive.

Refocus Line: "I don't want to overwhelm you, so let me ask — what's the one thing on your mind right now about this opportunity? Let's focus there."

For someone who prioritises feeling understood, this line conveys empathy and reassurance.

Permission to Move Forward: "Does this feel like a good fit so far? Would you like to take the next step, [like attending a meeting or watching a video]?"

5. Playful and Light-hearted

Opening Line: "Hi [Prospect's Name], this is [Your Name]. I saw you left your details for more info about [topic/product], so I thought I'd call and save you from endless Googling! Got a minute to chat?"

This playful approach sets a relaxed tone and makes the conversation feel enjoyable right from the start.

Transition from Chit-Chat Line: "Alright, enough about me — I'm sure you didn't leave your details just to hear my life story! Let's get into how [topic/product] might be just what you're looking for."

This playful transition keeps things light while steering the focus back to the prospect's needs.

Uncover the Pain Point Line: "So, what's the scoop? What got you thinking about [topic/opportunity]? Was there a specific moment when you thought, 'This could be what I need'?"

This line helps the prospect open up in a casual, pressure-free way, keeping the tone upbeat.

Refocus Line: "Okay, let's bring it back—if you had a magic wand, what's the one thing you'd change about your current situation?"

For the easy-going prospect who enjoys a bit of humour, this line lightens the mood.

Permission to Move Forward: "Does this sound like something that could work for you? Should we move to the next step, [like attending a meeting or watching a video]?"

6. Professional and Credible

Opening Line: "Hi [Prospect's Name], this is [Your Name]. I noticed you requested more information about [topic / product]. I'd love to provide you with all the details and answer any specific questions you have. Is now a good time?"

This professional tone sets the stage for a straightforward and productive conversation.

Transition from Chit-Chat Line: "It's been great chatting so far. Shall we shift gears and take a closer look at how [topic/product] works and how it could help you achieve your goals?"

This structured transition appeals to their preference for clarity and actionable insights.

Uncover the Pain Point Line: "To help me give you the most relevant information, could you share what specifically led you to explore this opportunity? Is there a particular problem you're trying to solve or a goal you want to achieve?"

This question encourages a focused discussion about their own goals and challenges, helping you tailor the conversation effectively.

Refocus Line: "To refocus, let's go back to basics — what's the key outcome you're hoping this opportunity will help you achieve?"

For analytical and goal-oriented prospects, structure is key.

Permission to Move Forward: "Does this all make sense? Would you like to take the next step, [like attending a meeting or watching a video]?"

Final Thoughts

When a conversation veers off course, it's easy to feel stuck. But with a little finesse and an understanding of personality dynamics, you can guide the discussion back to its purpose.

Each of these lines is just a tool to help you connect with your prospect on their terms, uncover their motivations, and keep the dialogue flowing.

Remember, the key to great conversations is adaptability.

Know your prospect, adjust your approach, and keep moving forward—because that's where the magic happens.

And for those occasions where it explodes and you feel you have got egg all over your face, remember this quote as you remove the metaphorical yolk from your hair, and prepare for the next prospect call.

> *"You can't say the wrong thing to the right person, and you can't say the right thing to the wrong person."* – Big Al

Chapter 11: Understanding Prospects' 'Why'

"If you know the why, you can endure any how."
— Friedrich Nietzsche

Why the why is necessary

Understanding a prospect's "why" is crucial because it reveals what truly motivates them—whether it's financial freedom, more time with family, or personal growth. When you know their driving force, you can tailor your message to show how your opportunity aligns with their goals.

Without this insight, you're just guessing, and a one-size-fits-all approach rarely resonates. Their "why" is the key to building trust and creating a genuine connection, which lays the foundation for long-term success.

Uncovering a prospects real why is a vital skill you must develop if you are going to build a big business. It will enable you to help a prospect come to a decision after glimpsing what their future could look like.

When you create the "full picture" for your prospect, it will allow them to see that a potential bright future really does exist. It should also show them, that it is within their grasp, that they can do it.

You make it obvious that you have a simple system that will enable them to succeed from where they are right now. It will transform their efforts into success if followed properly.

So many guides on recruiting say get their "why" as if it is some kind of thing that you can actually grasp. If you think of it as some inanimate object that you can just pluck out of thin air, you relegate the significance of their why.

Their personal "why" is a complex, volatile, ever-changing mix of the desire to attain something and the fear that comes from wanting to avoid something, all bound up with the competing push and pull of wanting to please themselves whilst simultaneously trying not to upset others.

Often your prospect will be unsure of the "real" why, so your role is to attempt to gain a superficial understanding – A direction of travel not a specific destination.

Most amateurs fail to see that it not just getting a "why" to fill in a tick box. The real power of professionally discovering a prospect's why is not limited to the benefit of actually knowing the real answer.

Its true power lies in the journey the two of you embark on and complete together. The bond that this mental journey creates is fundamental to building the long-term trust that sustains a new business during those moments of struggle and trust me, from all of my experience I can guarantee there will be moments, many moments of struggle in both your futures.

It's this process your prospect goes through as they display their vulnerability to you, when they share their true hopes and fears for the future. It cements the bonds of trust and faith that will be remembered long after the current "why" has been achieved or dropped.

Failing to take your prospect on this journey of discovery purely for your own convenience is the height of amateurish behaviour – **DON'T DO IT.**

Develop the strength to be out of your comfort zone and be a professional that always builds for the long term.

If your prosect does not get the opportunity to unpack their past journey to their present position with all the obstacles and successes, in THEIR mind the solution you propose cannot be trustworthy as it did not take everything fully into account so is likely to fail.

You personally may not need to hear the "story," but your prospect needs to tell it in full. If they are reluctant and hesitate in sharing their current situation in full, but you move forward just because you want a sign up, you have not followed our system, nor I would argue have you done anyone a long-term favour, especially yourself.

The future is now built on sand, not a firm foundation. You could throw the kitchen sink at supporting them, and they will just fade away, leaving you feeling disappointed and used because you worked hard for this recruit, and they abandoned you.

Reality check. It's your fault if you try to skip or take short cuts with this critical part of the process – *It's always all about them, not what is comfortable or easy for you.*

Prospects who have the inner resolve needed to build a great business must be given the opportunity to take their time in assessing what you have to offer. Remember they could join any business, anywhere.

So, pay them the respect and get to the full picture, again this is not to be a nosey busy body, it's to enable you as a professional to frame your opportunity in the best possible, authentic light for them to appreciate the potential for them.

Let me give you a great example of just assuming things without taking the time to actually check those assumptions are valid.

It was whilst on the campaign trail for a parliamentary by-election.

Picture the scene. The candidate was a few houses behind, as the main group with his election agent were now chatting with another household further along the street. After a few minutes he catches up, arriving at the front door, he is ushered in to meet someone who'd love to see him.

In his haste he whizzes past the cards which were placed all around the room, into the back room where he discovers an elderly gentleman in a chair surrounded by his family. "Who's the lucky birthday boy!" the candidate bellowed.

The room fell silent, you know that tumbleweed silence. Eventually the silence was broken by the voice of a frail old lady in what can only be described as a whispered shout, as she corrected him "It's a wake not a birthday party."

If ever there was a reason to never make a basic assumption let this be it.

How do we get people to tell us their current situations? Sometimes the driving reason for seeking change is held so privately not even their husband, wife or best friend are aware of its existence.

The foundation is trust!

It is critical that you apply yourself, sensitively to this task. You are seeking to create an environment where your prospect will, having seen how professional you are, have sufficient faith in you to share their current problems and their vision for the future.

Remember, they might avoid sharing the true reason as it may, in their mind, be too embarrassing to share.

Often prospects withhold the key detail as they feel revealing it will confirm the fact that they have failed themselves or even more frequently failed their family.

This is a journey, that with experience you will get better at navigating. However, let me be brutally clear – YOU will only get better if you start. The only way to master this skill is by repeated practice.

A great question! In 3 years time we meet up to celebrate. I've got the champagne on ice. I pour into the glasses, and as we clink, I say "congratulations, you did it!" – **What would you love us to be celebrating?**

Part 4

Sustaining Follow-Up Over Time

Chapter 12: Creating Early Success

Remember, for you the emotional engagement or buzz is when they "join." But for them it's when they start to see results.

Ensuring Early Wins for New Starters

A new starter's journey in any endeavour is often defined by the experiences they encounter in their first few weeks. Early wins — those small, achievable successes — can serve as the foundation for confidence, motivation, and long-term commitment. Our role, as mentors and guides, is to structure the path to ensure these wins are not only possible but inevitable.

The Importance of Early Wins

Starting something new can be overwhelming. There's a steep learning curve, a barrage of new information, and often, the nagging doubt of "can I really do this?"

Early wins combat this doubt. They provide immediate evidence of progress and capability. Each win, no matter how small, is a reminder: "Yes, you can."

By celebrating these wins, we reinforce positive behaviour and set a tone of encouragement and support. It's about creating momentum, a ripple effect that transforms initial effort into sustained success.

Designing Early Wins

To ensure early wins, we must:

1. **Set clear, achievable goals**: Break down larger objectives into bite-sized tasks.

2. **Provide focused support**: Offer guidance and resources tailored to their starting point.

3. **Celebrate progress**: Recognise and reward even the smallest accomplishments.

Practical Examples

Reaching out to their warm market: A new starter in a direct selling business might initially feel daunted by the idea of reaching out to potential customers or recruits.

Instead of asking them to cold-call strangers, begin with their warm market of friends, family, or acquaintances like work colleagues, who already trust them.

A win could be as simple as securing one product order or arranging one introductory conversation.

When Tom, one of our new starters, got his first "yes" from a family friend, we celebrated by sharing his success both on his Facebook wall, with the aim of getting some other friends to support him as well as in our team Facebook Group. This not only boosted Tom's confidence but also inspired others to take similar steps.

First Public Post: Encourage a new starter to make a short, authentic social media post about their journey. This doesn't have to be perfect; the goal is simply to share their excitement.

The "win" might be the number of likes, comments, or even a private message of support they receive. This small action builds their confidence in sharing their story.

When Sarah posted about why she joined our team, she received three comments from friends asking for more information. We cheered her on and discussed strategies for following up.

Here are some ideas for early wins to celebrate, but you can find thousands.

- Their first social media post sharing their new journey.
- Generating 5 prospects.
- Booking their first appointment or consultation.
- Sending out their first personalised message to a potential customer.
- Receiving their first "yes" to a product or service offer.

- Completing their first online training or module.
- Participating in their first team meeting or call.
- Sharing their "why" story with the team or on social media.
- Making their first follow-up call.
- Posting their first product review or testimonial.
- Reaching a small milestone, like $150 of sales

Celebrating Success: *Celebration is key. It validates effort, fosters belonging, and motivates further action. Whether it's a public shoutout, a small gift, or a personal message of congratulations, recognition amplifies the impact of early wins.*

As leaders, we have the power to shape a new starter's narrative. By engineering moments of success and celebrating them wholeheartedly, we pave the way for not just short-term wins but a long-term journey of growth and achievement.

Help them get results immediately by doing XX and YY before the end of the day.

What little great news story can you engineer tonight? Do you have a sale or recruit in the pipeline that you can pass to your new starter, using it as both a training piece and an authentic reason for celebrations?

Do you have a short training they can attend and get a personalised certificate, that they can proudly share on social media? Again it could be a great early win on their first day, what a fantastic opportunity for a celebration.

But it's just a little certificate, I hear you say! If that's your view then we have some extra work to do, right here, right now.

Question: How many times in the average prospect's day at work did their boss say, something like "You smashed it today, I have a really good feeling about your future. In fact, I'm certain now you've gained your first certificate after only a couple of hours"?

Well, with all my experience, I'd have an educated guess, that it would be somewhere close to, absolutely never.

So, if we can create a genuine reason for celebrating and uplifting people we are fulfilling our role as professionals.

Think of it in the opposite way, the trigger for most arguments is something tiny. Most people readily accept this hypothesis, but because of their inbuilt bias they choose not to acknowledge the opposite, namely that tiny little things can be the trigger for effort to be put into great achievements.

If your new team member experiences success on their first day, they'll go to bed feeling inspired, envisioning a promising future. However, if they don't see any positive results, they'll lie awake, plagued by doubts and fears that they've made a mistake by joining. After all, they've invested their money and gained nothing but uncertainty. To make matters worse, they might also face criticism from a sceptical partner who questions their decision, accusing them of falling for a scam and insisting that no one earns real money that way.

Whilst we are talking about early success let me address one common error that inexperienced leaders often make, as a result of genuinely trying to do the best for their new recruit.

When you get a new recruit, make it your mission not to overwhelm them with detail. They do not need to know how to process a return at this stage. I know this is a certainty as they are yet to make a sale.

It is also overkill to run through all the details of your pay plan along with every bonus that is on offer. Instead explain what their first step or next step should be. Simple focus is the key.

Keep the new information to a bare minimum. Focus on what they need to know for the next step. Never more than the next **THREE** steps or actions they need to take. Once they have accomplished that one step, you can move on to the next batch of actions.

For those who say they want to know everything now, reassure them that you will be there to answer all their questions, as they progress - "we can cover that when you have done [a sale / attended the quick start training /

generate an inquiry], if I covered it today it would not make much sense."

Trust me when it comes to training a new starter successfully, less I definitely more.

Chapter 13: Keeping the Pot Simmering

You have to create a roaring fire to bring what needs to be a huge pot to the boil, and then use measured heat to keep that pot simmering.

This chapter is the one that will make the difference between having a good business and having a great business that transforms your entire life.

> *"The best prospects are often the ones who say no at first but continue to watch and listen."* - Big Al

Everyone knows the best wines aren't the ones bottled last week — they're the ones that have been carefully nurtured, aged with patience and given time to develop their full flavour and character.

Similarly, successful follow-ups aren't about rushing; they're about consistent care and attention over time. Just like great wine, building relationships and trust with your prospects takes time, but the results are worth the wait.

Rhythm is key here; you are seeking to create a rhythm that carries you along at a great pace even when you don't quite feel up to it.

Think about your music playlists. There is probably a high tempo one with loads of beats per minute to help with the gym or exercise. Then there's the background one for when you are looking to bury yourself in intense work.

Your business rhythm or pulse needs to have a number of different tones, or you'd just be a monotonous flatline.

Business works in waves. By creating a constant stream of small waves, you are building the momentum that will eventually develop into a tsunami of business growth.

From countless studies and my own empirical observations, there are **three** different time frames needed to establish momentum, creating and sustaining the rhythm of growth.

Weekly

The focus here is on the foundational activities — are you doing the basics? Did you generate prospects and follow them up? This is where the groundwork is laid, and the first week of contact with new prospects is the most critical.

The frequency and intensity of follow-up's will naturally diminish as time passes, but consistency during this initial phase is non-negotiable. Weekly tasks are the engine of your business, and no matter what else is happening, they must be done.

These are your non-negotiables — the actions that keep the momentum alive, ensuring a steady stream of new prospects.

Quarterly

The 90-day period feels inherently right—it aligns with every rhythm, from the natural flow of the seasons to the pulse of man-made financial systems, like quarterly VAT returns.

Jim Rohn said it best: *"Measurable progress in reasonable time."* Quarterly reviews are the right time frame to step back and assess the bigger picture, but they don't replace the weekly tasks—they run alongside them.

Each quarter builds on the last, but the foundational work of generating and following up with new prospects must continue. Think of it as layering: the weekly grind fuels the quarterly growth, and without it, progress stalls. *Analysis equals paralysis*, so keep moving forward by focusing on clear, actionable steps.

Annually

The year's Big Message is about setting the tone and aligning everything with your mission.

Your mission serves as the background melody, the deeper reason that keeps you grounded. Annual reflection is about assessing the cumulative impact of your weekly and quarterly efforts.

Did your consistent foundational work pay off? Have you stayed true to your mission while continuously generating new prospects?

This reflection isn't just about outcomes; it's about ensuring the layers of weekly, quarterly, and annual actions are building toward something meaningful.

Remember, your mission fuels your *why*—and that's the difference between thriving and just getting by.

Chapter 14: Comprehensive Follow-Up Framework

This system is designed to engage prospects, understand their needs, and guide them through exploring a side hustle opportunity.

They may well be considering other options, from selling on eBay to getting a part-time bar job.

Your role is to work out if your opportunity is a good fit, either now or by staying connected, as it may be a great fit sometime in the future.

It is not a single event, it is a drip, drip process over an extended period.

It leverages multiple touchpoints and different team promotional assets, delivered in many different ways for maximum long-term impact.

I must stress the aim of this system is NOT to get a prospect to join on the first contact. Think about it, we are offering a business partnership, like a business marriage. Would you ever think it acceptable to ask someone to marry you, after a single 45 second phone call.

Look, if someone wants to join and give it a go, of course, you are not going to turn them away, but you must see this as a consequence of the process, it is certainly not the most desirable outcome. Why do I say that, well from personal experience across many decades, I can tell with a huge degree of confidence that:

Prospects who join on a whim quit on a whim.

Your long-term business strategy must include discovering, nurturing and a commitment to remain connected to, as many prospects as possible.

Week in week out a random prospect, from this ever-expanding pool of talent, will surprise you by seeking you out and joining, as on that day, their world will be different than it was two months ago, six months ago, or even a year ago.

When it's their moment – you must have created a background awareness that directs them straight to you. They chose you because you have demonstrated your helpful and professional attitude throughout the follow-up process.

Because of your constant attention to this follow-up process you have created a brand that surrounds you. It is your brand, a brand that will shout trustworthy. It will scream you are likeable and helpful, and your prospect will see you as a friend.

By now we all know, who prospects join with? **They join with people they KNOW, LIKE & TRUST.**

Need I say more?

There are four distinct phases:

- **Discovery and Initial Contact (Days 1 –7)**
- **Nurturing Relationship (Weeks 2 –4)**
- **Maintaining Engagement (Months 1 – 3)**
- **Long-Term Connection (Months 4 – 12+)**

Obviously, there is a much greater frequency in the contact attempted in the first few weeks. This gently tails off until it becomes a few times a year.

Before we delve into the specifics, we really must talk about the different methods of contact, as there is a definite pecking order when it comes to how you contact your prospect.

I go back to marriage again. Paint me a picture of any young man or woman, visualising how their loved one will propose to them?

Let me make some guesses. It's a romantic scene, their beloved is down on one knee, the jewellery box is open, and the ring is on display.

I think we are all on the same page here about what this would look like in most people's versions with all their unique little fantasy woven into the rich tapestry.

Now let me ask, did anyone have as their vision, the proposal coming as email to your work's email address, nothing else, no romance, no ring?

The other truly important thing missing in this email scenario is the jeopardy, the absolute vulnerability of kneeling there in front of someone, looking into their eyes and waiting what seems like an age for their response.

There can be no doubt that, especially in the first few contacts the choice of communication method, has to be live, ideally in person, then as a video call and finally, as a phone call.

These live interactions help enormously. They allow you to use non-verbal clues when you are trying to build a full picture of the prospect you are working with.

Sometimes people say one thing with words but portray a completely different message with tone and body language.

Let me describe an example of this. When you return home and ask your partner how they are, and they respond with "FINE" – you **hear** the word; you know what it means in the dictionary, but every part of your brain is screaming, he or she is absolutely anything but fine.

To me the message is as clear as day; wherever possible connect with prospects via a live call as opposed to written text.

One final point on sharing the assets and sending invitations to real world events or online webinars to your prospects, never prejudge. You must treat your prospects as independent adults and allow them to make their own decisions. **Never decide for them.**

If you ever hear yourself say "I won't send a link to her, as she never attends" you now know you are making an error of judgement, just send it and let them choose.

Right, let's take a look at each phase in a little more detail.

Phase 1: Discovery and Initial Contact (Days 1–7)

Aim: To fully understand the prospect's needs, introduce them to the opportunity, and encourage engagement.

Day 1 - Follow-Up Call - Share your personal story about why you started your side hustle and how it has impacted your life. Invite them to take a short quiz: 'Are You Ready for a Side Hustle?' Include a link to an upcoming team Opportunity Presentation or the Weekly Workshop.

Day 2 – Send a *Welcome Email with Quiz or Opportunity Invitation* - Mention the quiz or opportunity session shared in the email. Ask an open-ended question like, 'What attracted you to exploring a side hustle?

Day 3 - Send a Story Email (Other People's Stories) - Share 1–2 inspiring stories from team members who found success with their side hustle. Include a call-to-action: "what would you like your story to say?, Let's chat one-on-one!"

143

Day 5 - *Personal Message plus a Newspaper Resource* - Send a personalised text or social media message: 'Hi [Name], I thought this article from our team newspaper might interest you. It explains how a side hustle like ours can fit into busy lives like yours!' Include the link or attach the article.

Day 7 - *Invitation to a 1-2-1 Session* - Offer to meet one-on-one to explore their current situation and side hustle options. Highlight that this session is a no-pressure call, focused on helping them decide if this business is right for them.

Years ago, we thought we were so cutting edge, we had autoresponders that would whizz off emails at specific times. These just seemed to fall out of fashion.

Let me tell you that these are making a big come back, but with a major difference; it is no longer acceptable for the sequence to be just a stream of emails.

These sequences are a blend of contact methods, with a mix of asset types, delivered in different settings or online platforms.

Whereas, it used to be a stream of robotic emails that fired off in turn, today's more professional process could see a phone call today, a video sent by messenger tomorrow, a newsletter emailed over the weekend and a business article shared on LinkedIn next week.

Phase 2: Nurturing Relationships (Weeks 2–4)

Aim: To build trust, provide more information, and gently guide them to explore further.

Week 2 - *Follow-Up Email Highlighting Team Success* - Share a success story from the team, to showcase the collective credibility and results. Reinforce the invitation to join the next Weekly Workshop or book a Side-Hustle Options Session.

Week 3 - *Social Media Engagement* - Comment on or share relevant posts by the prospect. Post team updates or a personal win related to your side hustle, tagging them if appropriate.

Week 4 - *Check-In Call or SMS to ask:* 'Have you had a chance to explore the side hustle options we discussed? I'd love to help answer any lingering questions!'

Phase 3: Maintaining Engagement (Months 1–3)

Aim: Keep your prospect warm and showcase your commitment to always providing ongoing value. Always feel comfortable about giving an invitation to an event repeatedly.

Month 1 - *Educational Email (Newspaper + Workshop)* - Share an article from the team newspaper about overcoming challenges in starting a side hustle. Invite them to the next Weekly Workshop or schedule a follow-up 1-2-1.

Month 2 - 'Are You Ready Now?' *Check-In* - call or message to ask if their situation has changed or if they're ready to explore further. Share a quick update about team growth or recent successes.

Month 3 - Success Story Email with Side-Hustle Options Reminder - Highlight a new, specific story that matches their situation. Reinvite them to a Side-Hustle Options Session tailored to their interests.

Phase 4: Long-Term Connection (Months 4 to 12 and beyond)

Aim: To keep the prospect engaged and aware of your long-term commitment to help – They need to know you'll be willing to welcome them when they are ready. You need to demonstrate patience. The timing of any start will always be in their hands. Remember, our role is to continually open the "door" to our opportunity, it's not for us to get irritated when prospects choose not to walk through it. We just try opening it in a few weeks or months.

Quarterly - Touchpoints (Email and Call) - Send updates on team milestones, new opportunities, or changes in side-hustle options. Offer a free resource, like a productivity planner for side hustlers.

Bi-Annual - Exclusive Event Invitation - Invite them to a special online team event or mastermind session to enable them to see the team community spirit in action.

146

Annual - *Holiday Card or Personalised Note* - Send a handwritten card reflecting on their progress, such as "how did the move go", and once again demonstrating your ongoing willingness to help.

Remember, this is just a guide to the timing and the delivery method. I know people don't really like the fact that there is not a single "right way." They miss the certainty a right way would provide.

However, I can give you a different certainty, **the details just do not matter.** The only thing that matters is that you do something, with one of these assets on or around these key dates.

I like to think of it as using "shuffle" on my play list, the exact order is not critical as long as I still get to experience all of my best tracks.

Feeling a little overwhelmed?

If right now you are thinking, "but I don't do any of this!" Then, I am really happy for you, because you now have a guide to how you can make simple changes over time to *massively increase your effectiveness.*

This list is the grand master standard, if you are new or have just realised how important consistent follow-ups are.

Here is the key to implementing it; "**one step at a time**". Do not try to start all these contact points at once, build into them at a pace that suits you.

Start with your new prospects, and increase your contact with them, then when you have your first week process comfortably up and running, move to the quarterly and so on.

You can filter your old leads into this process as you go, remembering to obtain their ongoing consent as you progress.

One final point to help you overcome the lack of certainty in timing and asset choice, no one could ever know with any degree of confidence what would be the ideal item, to choose for a unique human being with all the other things happening in their world on any one day.

So, don't stress and pick one or if you like conformity, you can set your plan in stone. Make the decision once and then use that template for each and every prospect thereafter.

Oh, do you feel the power rushing to your head, this system is yours to own and control. You and you alone are responsible for its success.

Your prospect plays no part in you successfully following this process, because your success lies in simply carrying out the next action for every prospect professionally.

I have prepared a simple one-page tick sheet. It will help you have a system to keep track of your prospect's journey. It can be download it from: www.howardphilpott.com/downloads

Part 5:

The Master's Edge

Chapter 15: Expectation – Where Dreams go to Die

I have been fortunate to see some of the world's most successful recruiters at work, up close and personal. For them, following up is not a chore, it is one of the best parts of their business fundamentals. It is the part that brings the most excitement and new opportunity to grow.

Here is another nugget. I almost did not include it because it is what I genuinely believe to be the best explanation of why some people find following up easy and others run a mile to avoid picking up the phone. It is a simple philosophy, that can be expressed in just a single world – **expectation!**

This is a difficult attitude to adopt as it often runs contrary to our sense of natural justice. A great and common example is this:

Emily joins and makes all the "right noises" about wanting to build a great business, so you invest loads of time and effort into guiding and coaching her. You even pay for an advert to help accelerate her income growth.

Then out of the blue you get a text, "it's not for me" and she's blocked you. As you read her text, your response starts to build, relatively calmly at first, but then as you run though things in your head, the disappointment, gives way to frustration, which can evolve into anger, then it explodes into full blown RAGE.

Let me take you on this journey in more detail. I'm interested to see if any of these chime with you as something you have experienced personally or in your team.

The disappointment: This stems from your feeling "she was going to be the one," the one that transforms your fortunes and now she's gone – your future looks bleak.

The frustration: Is based on the fact it's just not "fair." I invested in her and she's just dropped me! – why does this always happen to me?

The anger: You look for confirmation that you have been wronged to fuel this growing anger, "I did nothing wrong; she's just used me."

The RAGE: You and your "chimp" (Dr Steve Peters – The Chimp Paradox) – The "chimp" is the old survival part of our brain that controls the fight or flight response and can overwhelm our more rational thinking brain. You are now in full jungle rampage mode. The conversation in your head regarding this is now shouting – "How could she? And she couldn't even be bothered to pick up the phone and tell me, she sent a text, after all I've done for her!" - [read the book]

All of this emotional turmoil is avoidable.

The next sentence is a personal philosophy. It is really short but it's power to help you build the mental resilience to stay in the game long enough to build a great business is enormous.

The key: *I genuinely believe in everyone's potential; But I have no expectation that they will realise it.*

Right now, I'd be giving you the "sentence" *(see page 26)* before I give you what I think is the key to mental survival in this industry.

> *You need to accept that what any other person does is not in your control, it is theirs. Period.*

Now reviewing the Emily situation:

Disappointment: Having put your expectation that Emily would fulfil her potential, and build your business, she didn't. She tried it, and it did not work out. It intrigues me how many leaders promote their opportunity as a way to freedom and then get all indignant when people exercise that freedom and leave.

The frustration: My mum, who sadly passed away when I was still at high school, had a saying that is so appropriate for this situation, "who told you life was fair"

Now assuming you did nothing to drive Emily away, you should not get frustrated as this only has one outcome, you and your business suffer. The way to handle this perceived unfairness is to take a wider perspective.

Emily is one of those people who fit the "tried it and left" box.

As a point of interest, she definitely does not belong in the "I never started" box, and we don't yet know if she could belong in the "I came back to it" box.

Our role is to sort people into the box they choose for themselves, after we have professionally given them all information we can.

It is *definitely not* our role to force people into a box they are not ready or destined for.

This is a critical concept to understand, we are not in the business to pressure people into making snap decisions or to do something that they are not ready for, especially if that pressure is motivated by our personal self-interest.

Obviously, we are here to encourage people who are unsure if it is for them, to give it a try, then make an informed decision.

Do not be like a young child trying to force a round peg into a triangle shaped hole.

The anger: Now, assuming you did nothing to drive Emily away, you should not carry the emotional baggage of her choices. Instead, accept them and ensure that you create an environment for her to return in the future and fulfil the potential you have seen.

As an analogy consider this: A lighthouse provides guidance to ships, but it can't control which vessels respond to its light. In MLM, you share your opportunity like the lighthouse shines its light. If you expect everyone to "dock at your harbour," disappointment will follow. Your role is to illuminate, not to steer every ship.

The Rage: This one is all on you! When someone cuts you up by changing lanes right in front of you, as you drive to the supermarket. The incident itself, lasted for just a few seconds, but you get to choose whether your reaction lasts for a few more seconds or you allow your reaction to destroy your whole day.

Can you control your response? Can you limit the impact? I believe you can. The way to do this is through personal choice.

There is no way of knowing the "background story."

Let's explore two plausible background stories:

1. The lady who cut you up had just had a call telling her that her 91-year-old mum has had a fall and pushed the panic button she wore around her neck, so she was driving aggressively as she wanted to get there to help as a matter of urgency.

2. The lady was just an inconsiderate, selfish t$@t, who doesn't care about other road users.

If you were somehow aware that it was story 1, would you have just let her in and wished her mum all the best?

How would your day have been after that? My expectation is that you'd feel uplifted, your selfless act of enabling her to respond quickly to the crisis, would have made you feel good.

Here's my point. The incident "you getting cut up" is identical in both stories. It's your reaction alone that decides if you sacrifice a whole day of your life to a "trivial" event.

There is another point that I can't resist making here.

Returning to the original frustration, a lot of it was rooted in the emotional reaction triggered by "and she didn't call, she just sent an SMS or text".

So many people are oblivious to an unintended hypocrisy.

Consider this: how often do we justify our own choices by assuming others will understand? In the above situation, you were upset because someone didn't call, they only texted. You then perceive that as a slight. You feel you were not valued sufficiently.

Yet, when it comes to reaching out to prospects, do you catch yourself thinking, "It's fine, they won't want a call; I'll just send a quick text?"

The disconnect here is subtle but powerful. We crave the investment of effort and attention from others but often hesitate to offer the same in return.

Recognising this contradiction is the first step toward aligning your actions with the empathy you expect.

The Serenity Prayer and Follow-Ups:

The Serenity Prayer offers wisdom that can help navigate the emotional rollercoaster of follow-ups:

" grant me the serenity to accept the things I cannot change, courage to change the things I can, and wisdom to know the difference."

When dealing with prospects, some will respond, and others won't—and that's beyond your control.

What you *can* control is how you approach each follow-up, choosing to act with persistence. You can also control how you react to a follow-up by electing to handle it with grace while letting go of frustrations.

This mindset not only keeps you grounded but also ensures that every interaction stems from clarity and purpose rather than emotional highs and lows.

Chapter 16: The Integrity of Follow-Ups

"Exercise integrity in the moment of choice."

Every tiny choice builds on the previous one, every choice is shaping the scale of business you will have. These choices are not independent of one another, they form a chain, a chain that will anchor your business when it gets difficult (and it will get difficult).

Think of each separate decision as a moment when you have two doors in front of you, one of which is a great big heavy door with a huge star with the words "BIG BUSINESS" across it, the other is a plain, ordinary door with a dull sign that reads "poor business."

From now on, you know that every choice you make about your business is not tiny or irrelevant, because you are now acutely aware that each tiny decision is building a habit, your habit of whether you are going to push for a BIG or poor business.

Hey, I'm not judging, that's your job – but I am pointing out to you, don't blame anyone or anything else. You as an adult must own the consequences of your everyday choices.

The act of reading this book, will not deliver a big business for you unless you CHOOSE to take action and inspire others to do the same. I know it will feel uncomfortable but just go do it anyway.

Here are some examples of critical moments, always be on red alert for these moments.

- Every minute you claim to be "at work" then actually show up and take the actions that add value.

- When a prospect call is due, then make that call.

- Every blog or article that should be shared, go share it.

- Every newsletter that has to be written, sit and write it.

Deep down, you always know what the "right" action is, but when you don't feel like doing it, you start saying things like "it won't matter."

When you hear yourself justify the wrong action, just ask yourself what would your business icon or mentor do? Then follow that guidance, even though it came from you, because you do really know.

Success comes from the consistent and relentless pursuit of *actually doing* these *"Professional Follow-ups."*

"Do not mistake movement with achievement."
Jim Rohn

Conclusion

Success will surely come if you adopt the follow-up professionals' philosophy and system. Then act upon it for as long as it takes:

- *Once a prospect has self-identified* – I will always stay in touch until they tell me not to. I will gain permission to keep them updated and deliver useful content.
- I will share tips and ideas to help make life better, this is one way I can show I really care about my prospects.
- I will be patient and wait for them - if not now, tomorrow, next week or even the next decade - I will always be ready to welcome them

It really is that simple. Then when the moment is right for them, I will be the trusted one they contact. *True attraction.*

You are already all you need to be capable of truly stellar performance. To build huge and lasting success, all you have to do is choose to accomplish the next tiny task with a smile, before moving onto the next, and the next, and the next . . . .

"the only route to true freedom is through disciplined actions"

Act with integrity,
make the correct decision,
especially when alone,
and you will be
unstoppable X

Notes

Notes

Notes

Printed in Great Britain
by Amazon

60218844R00097